"*The Rose Knight* takes readers
One reads like a lost Bible Canc
that hits very close to home. *Th*   ～ ～ you by the heart
and simply won't let go until you finish. Anaiya's storytelling
transports you into another mystical dimension, one that demands
your undivided attention."

—HEATHER STRANG, AUTHOR OF *THE QUEST* SERIES

"A powerful storyteller with a passionate imagination, Anaiya Sophia
ignites a gentle yet effulgent light as she guides the reader through her
words in a journey of discovery. *The Rose Knight* is a fantastical
meeting of 'Sophia' in our modern-day."

—ROSAMONDE MILLER

THE ROSE KNIGHT

Part One: Sophia's Story

ANAIYA SOPHIA

ISBN 978-1-291-56262-0

First published 2014

Text © Anaiya Sophia 2014

To send correspondence to the author of this book contact her directly at

www.anaiyasophia.com

Cover art by

Jo Jayson

www.jojayson.com

Cover design and typesetting by

David Andor / Wave Source Design

www.wavesourcedesign.com

To my Beloved, in all your many faces

Acknowledgements

To my parents, Dinah and Patrick Cuddihy, for the greatest gift that can be given. The gift of knowing your passions and watching you effortlessly embody them gave me the inspiration and permission to do the same. I love you both so much.

To my beloved Luc-Tibor Erdos, who steadfastly supported me on every level as I wrote this book. Thank you for building this life with me, and showing me that this love can be lived.

To my passionate and magical midwife and editor, Jenna Paulden, thank you so much for injecting your juice and insight into the creation of *The Rose Knight*.

To Jo Jayson for the use of your Magdalene on the front cover (www.jojayson.com).

To David Andor for the outstanding design of this book.

To Len and Margaret Cole, for truly bringing this story alive.

To Shmeymi Padma AO for working together on Part One and the encouragement to dream BIG...

To Rosamonde Miller, from whose copyrighted work I have quoted extensively in giving voice to my characters, especially the Sophia, as well as in ways that cannot be spoken...

Lastly, to all of you who played your role so supremely in the creation of *The Rose Knight*.

Author's Note

The Rose Knight is the first part of a trilogy that enlightens modern readers about the ancient mythos of Sophia, Goddess of Wisdom. The second part of the trilogy, *Return of the Grail King*, continues where *The Rose Knight* left off, but this time through the eyes of the Logos, the masculine embodiment of the Divine. The final part, Hieros Gamos, is the coming together of Sophia and the Logos in every sense of the word! For it is this time that we are all currently partaking in, as the Divine has its way with us and humanity awakens into the great Rebirth.

   This is a work of fiction, although the imaginary characters do exist. It was inspired during one helluva dark night of the soul. During this time, I had to reach deep into my being for something primordial to hold onto, and there I found Her glistening in the black light—the Holy Sophia, the Mother of all creation. She promptly propelled me into the Gnostic Gospels, particularly the Pistis Sophia itself. Within a few pages, I realized that I was living Sophia's story, that I recognized the characters (rather too well) and that this was a universal tale. As I continued to read, I became immersed in the material so deeply that I moved into a realm of transmission that was teeming with life and available for all who desired to enter.

Reeling with enthusiasm, I spoke of these works to my peers, encouraging them to read and open to receive the gnosis. To my dismay, they came back to me with the same response: I don't get it, its too heavy, it's too complicated, it's too much ... And so I set out upon my quest to retell the story with modern day language and current levels of consciousness. At first I did not realize that to tell this tale, I had to live it fully, embody it and make it my own. Many times the writing would stop because I could go no further. Then the next piece would be lived, retrieved and integrated—so onwards I would plough.

As you read this book, you will see, feel, and know that Sophia's story is your story, our story—everyone's story. *The Rose Knight Trilogy* is an inner journey and an outer portrayal of how I interpreted the Gnostic scriptures, and of my unfolding along the mystical path of Christ Consciousness. I do believe that it is this mystical element that will become one of the most essential forces necessary for the radical, revolutionary breakthrough that is already breathing down our necks. Many of us call this time the quickening, and we are feeling the edges of the old reality blur; the sand is shifting under our feet, but miraculously we are still held in the palm of Love. Because of this raining down of grace I can say with confidence that you will recognize the characters in this Trilogy. They are people that you have known, people you have loved and people you have cried over. At this moment, we all stand upon an evolutionary crossroads and I believe we are being urged to become active, impassioned midwives of this great revolutionary Rebirth.

So—that's my opinion. Now what's important is for you to feel your way through this story, to discover what inner doors open, what emotions are aroused and stirred, what insights may be revealed. I attempted to write *The Rose Knight* as a transmission rather than a story. The details are not important, the facts are definitely not important, and the linear unfolding of events—forget it! All that matters is your own response to the material.

Finally, although the story is based around actual events, this is a novel, and it is certainly not a "Spiritual How To." I have hinted at real events, real establishments and real scenarios to activate your own deep, inherent wisdom … Sophia Herself.

I wish you the most magnificent journey!

Anaiya Sophia

My other books include: *Sacred Sexual Union*, *Womb Wisdom* (Inner Traditions), *Pilgrimage of Love* and *Open your Heart with Kundalini Yoga*. I live in the Languedoc, Southern France, with my beloved Luc-Tibor. Together we run a small retreat space and B&B in Puivert called AmmaRosa where we can receive small groups and individuals who are interested in exploring Sacred France and all aspects of this work.

The exact nature of Sophia must be discovered, and like gnosis, can never be put into words, for it is never fully apprehended and held by the brain once the individual returns to ordinary consciousness. It can only be pointed at in the language of myth and poetry.

Nothing that is said about the myths about Sophia is to be taken literally. Gnostic myths need to be understood with a different mindset than the one used by religions that require literal beliefs.

Rosamonde Miller, Ecclesia Gnostica Mysteriorum, California
http://www.gnosticsanctuary.org/

In the beginning

Chapter 1

In the Beginning

Out of the Fullness came He, who, without speaking, yet spoke His name, and it was unknown to all but Him. And She, whose womb is the gateway to all the worlds.

Tender waves of pearlescent light danced upon Her face, framing the far reaches of Her gaze. With the rise and fall of Her bosom She orchestrated the tidal choirs of both heaven and earth. Galaxies spewed forth from Her Womb, organizing in perfect grace under the watchful eye of the Nameless One. Songs of supernal Light resounded between them, imbuing all of Creation with their love and embrace. Everything was in its rightful place; harmony unfurled Her wings and brought all unto Her fold.

Herein was perfection. Every nuance of His beauteous bride gladdened Him as unmeasured time passed through indefinable space. A glorious radiance suffused Her body. Droplets of light cascaded on Her brow; rivulets of radiance created Her hair; skin soft as moonlight blended into the dust of stars behind Her; rubies large as mountains formed Her hands; emeralds the size of Gaia glinted in Her eyes; jasper, sweet jasper, gleamed tenderly from Her womb, as the delicate curves of Her full breast heaved and shone starlight into the aching void.

Her face was born of alabaster, carved in pure pearl, clear and defined one moment, swathed in waves of light the next. Sometimes it dissolved, only to rise in swirling, coruscating spirals, dancing in delight, obeying Her every whisper of a thought; the subtlest shimmy of Her movement undulated Galaxies into manifestation.

Form followed form, light followed light; dancing motes of dust sparkled in Her twirling, grace-filled whirlwind; planets echoed across the universe in its wake. Silver shone from Her chin; moonbeams gleamed from Her ears, illuminating the darkness into its Truth. Sapphire robes bedecked Her one moment, crimson white the next, effortlessly, beguilingly shape shifting; for just as clothes are, so are forms.

He would often wander through the delightful ripples of Her presence, wishing to know Her more, aching to know this part of Him that encapsulated inexhaustible comeliness. She astounded Him. She filled His creation, stretching its boundaries at the seams, saturating His countless manifold realms with bursting ripeness and a glowing, intoxicating fragrance. She turned in Her dance to gaze back to Him, replete in Her glory, satiated in Her fullness, full of Herself.

In that moment, She had a thought, one that was born from separation. Realizing Her action, She quickly withdrew Her attention, but it was too late. Now, Her deep learning was about to begin.

Her body became clear as quartz; Her glorious luster now vanished into a transparent reverie. Millions upon millions of pieces shattered and came together, shattered and came together, millions upon millions of times, all in the same moment. A House of shattering light was born, a mansion of crossing, a bridge of becoming, a floating abyss of shining light resounding silently through infinity. A vague and distant shadow began to emerge on the horizon—a horizon that until this very moment had never even existed. Seeping into their entwined Divine consciousness, even when solitude naturally beckoned, they began to explore this burgeoning shadow, curious to know it's meaning, and yet hesitant to unlock its secret.

Alone, each One gazed into this nuance of unexplored possibility, a secret each kept without telling the other. It was only when the Holy Sophia was safely alone in Her inner sanctum that this shadowy companion chose its moment to silently, stealthily creep forward, pressing into Her awareness with a gradual, undulating momentum. This was the beginning of—something else.

Its presence overwhelmed Her. She had never known anything like it. Its incessant urgency to commune with Her threatened to envelope Her consciousness. She feared the magnitude of its message; the black pools of her irises swelled and a barely audible gasp escaped Her lips. It felt as if a distant, nostalgic sentiment grabbed at Her heart, aching for Her tenderness, begging for Her merciful embrace. She cried out aloud for the Nameless One; boundless and strange energies moved within Her as she held the shadow and its message.

In one movement, He was with Her. The Mother of all Creation, the Holy Sophia closed her eyes and rolled back into His buoyant Light, lolling in His sea of softly tinkling bells. Heaven rebounded from this colossal shifting of its Creators; for so long they had been the two pillars of the Temple--neither too far, nor too close, perfectly positioned to ensure balance and seamless perfection. The Nameless One placed His hand over Her heart, wordlessly instructing countless orbiting cherubs to swirl around them, incubating them from the rest of the Godhead.

He gazed into the eyes of the Holy Sophia, searching for the cause of Her effect, but all He encountered was the thunder of silence. A solitary tear claimed His attention as it aimlessly wandered across Her face. He felt wrenched when He saw into its substance. Captivated by its transmission, entranced by its beautiful agony, He held His Wife even closer. She began to rock back and forth, creating waves of movement that ricocheted throughout the heavens.

Something unforeseen was about to happen. But even this was not known. Yet.

Within the voluptuous rhythms of Sophia, a sea of sensation began to gather momentum, causing Her to swell and expand beyond space. With voluminous eyes, She turned to face the Nameless One, transmitting Her feeling instantaneously, "My Love, what is happening? I can feel our children calling me from afar."

The Nameless One responded. Gathering His Light into a spearhead, He condensed all infinity into one arcing flame of magnificence. With this single, solitary point, He penetrated Sophia, plunging the depths of Her mystery. She gasped, and Her head flew back to accommodate His brilliance, as He soared through Her chambers, both secret and revealed. Like an unyielding fiery phoenix, He swooped down into Her, determined to vanquish Her suffering. Again and again, He climbed to the heights of Her majesty, seeking answers, seeking a beckoning Truth. An urgency bit at His heels as He recalled how the She had looked at Him. He had never seen that haunted appearance in Her face before, and its memory scoured His heart.

His Living Light shone throughout Her landscape, causing deep bellowing moans to pour forth from Her lips. She delighted in His excavations, wanting him, yearning for Him to penetrate Her more, to find the places even He didn't know. Yet, though He searched and searched, He found nothing. With a reluctant rasp, He concentrated His Light and re-emerged outside Her.

"I could not find anything," He whispered, as He dropped His head and turned His back on Her. Disappointed that He could not help Her, and diminished from the almighty exertion, He walked away. Then, like a thunderous bolt of lightening, He struck his wings together to implode Himself back into the Pleroma, the Throne of Heaven.

She watched His Light begin to permeate other dimensions, leaving Her alone. She rolled into a deep abyss, saddened He could not find the cause of Her sorrow, aching and yearning because He had left Her inner sanctum. What was this incredible loneliness that swept through Her? How could She feel this empty when the whole Universe gyrated inside of Her? Closing Her eyes, the Holy Sophia turned inwards, into the deepest hidden folds of Her nature. There it was. She saw it, heard it.

It was a cry of many, many voices. "Please Mother, please help us!"

Chapter 2

The Descent

Platinum light perforated the nucleus of Her existence, its illumination renting the darkness all the way from Her subatomic worlds to the subterranean ones. Brandishing itself upon the veils that made up Creation, imprinting Glory in its wake, its platinum brilliance carved open a pathway deep inside Her womb. She reeled in bittersweet agony, howled in anguish, as She was pushed and pulled like a rag doll in the hands of squabbling children.

Undulating, circling roars of time and space torched Her ears, rebounding in thunder through the cavity of Her chest. She was being torn apart by the power of it. Beads of sweat ricocheted in every direction. Her convulsing head looked around for the source of this experience, and suddenly She sensed the agonizing suffering and cries of Her children. They were lost, they were coming undone, and something terribly, terribly horrific was happening to them. They were falling into darkness, a darkness so dense that it threatened to extinguish their connection to Her love.

Their cries echoed around Her, and like a compass needle, She felt an irresistible force working magically, magnetically, inexorably, to suck Her towards them without compunction, hesitation or delay. Her instincts, rich and inevitable, borne on a plethora of feelings, called out: "You have to do this! You must answer these prayers. Fall into your womb and attend to your children. Let go. Loosen your grip and allow your light to descend. Your children need you NOW!"

Her body began to bloat and stretch, elongating, raising like rubber. Her limbs inflated, and the air began to brighten and blur around Her, shifting in and out of myriad dimensions. Overtones whistled through Her ears, and piercing shards of multi-frequency sound filled Her head as it expanded into emptiness.

A deep, deafening rumble filled everything.

Myriads upon myriads of thoughts streamed gossamer-like through the canvas of Her mind, flinging themselves over Her like leaves blown aloft in a storm, like dust clouds in a twisting hurricane. Sucked of all air, thin and arid, She gasped into this vast, whirling maelstrom. Beyond, She could sense something even more tumultuous; a booming, ominous resonance of total, and utter, silence. A silence that intimated everything in a never ending well of nothingness. A silence like thunder.

She knew that silence. She had always known it.

"Oh Beloved Mother what is happening to us? Please help us!"

The wild cries tore at Her womb, begging Her to come forth and give way to the wildness within Her, and surrender to the instinctual, primal impulse to attend to Her children, no matter what the cost. There was nothing to hold onto, nothing to cling to. She released a blood-curdling shriek. Her cry mingled with the clamor of Her lost and agonized children, and the intensity of sound ripped through the gaping emptiness that separated them.

Paralyzed, She watched as a deep, fiery blaze filled Her womb. Gasping, she fell to Her knees, clutching Her belly. Already, unbeknownst to Her, Her Light was beginning to leave The Kingdom-Queendom, instinctively gravitating towards Her womb, like a spiraling trickle of water descending down a drain.

Her eyes rolled upwards into Her head. Taking an Almighty inhale, She sank down into Her sacrum, silently relinquishing all control. She could not bear this sorrowful torture a moment longer. With everything inside Her, She surrendered. Light, longing, tenderness, mercy, and protective feelings filled her, obliterating all else. Love filled Her with a burning, inconsolable urge that had to be obeyed.

With no thought whatsoever, the Queen of Heaven sounded into Her womb with unwavering sovereignty, '*I am coming, please, please hold on, I am coming. I will not abandon you. Not now, not ever!*'

Rotating rings of Light etched out a gateway within Her womb, a grand geometry that grew in magnetic power as every second passed. She squinted to fathom the configuration before Her, accessing all known geometries She had created in the past. Deafened by the silence it evoked, marveled by its majestic proportions, She realized its genesis was something unknown to Her, and yet strangely familiar. She felt drawn into the center of this grand portal: mesmerized, fascinated and pulled.

The cries of Her children intensified as the doorway became manifest.

Pushing against the edges of Heaven, She imploded in on Herself and dove through the new dimensional geometry She had created. Determined to reach the souls of Her children, She knew She had to go where no other Divine Soul had ever been—into the inky dark of nothingness. Like a comet She blazed a trail, pressing, pushing, unfurling in colossal undulating waves, boring apart the rippling tides of the un-manifest. All that remained were dissolving tendrils where Her Light had once been. And then … harrowing silence.

She fell.

Round and round and round She spun. Her body contorted and rotated, cycling faster and faster, caught in a washing machine on infinite spin. Bits of Her body melted off, crumbling and unraveling in Her wild and tumultuous orbit.

Spheres of diminishing Light, oceans of movement, and spirals of sound echoed as She fell. She descended through screeching wormholes of tumultuous passage, creating pathways and spirals of sound.

Then the *pressure* hammered against Her, pressing down Her soul, squeezing every particle and atom from Her being. All Light around Her faded and the darkness got heavier and heavier as She was catapulted head long into the next sphere, where the pressure increased and magnified. *Oh! Oh, the pressure! My light, My soul is diminishing!*

She managed to look out of the spin for a moment. The peace of the stars beckoned. She reached out, yet Her arm rapidly withered off, blown into stardust, effortlessly swept away by the massive waves of dark matter careering around Her.

She soared into yet another sphere, even denser than the last. She felt as if She was being strained, squeezed into a mould that was horrifyingly too small for Her. Every morsel, every drop of Her

Light was compressing in on itself. Gravity was boring into Her existence, transforming Her Divinity.

Her eyelids, or what was left of them, closed. She rolled back into the abyss. She dreamt She was in a black hole, dense and drawing Her down, down, down. Her only consciousness became infinite time enfolded in on itself, washing everything clean, so clean it no longer existed. So clean, *She* no longer existed.

There was no sound, no form, no Light, no body. Gone, gone, gone, everything gone.

Yet … within the heavy dark, a miniscule iota of light still burned. Yes, a seed of light flickered, faintly glowing amongst the parched aridity. She could not remember this Light, however, because the part of Her that could remember was already gone. Then from the nothingness, she emerged with a sickening thud. She fumbled in the dark.

"*Where am I!?*" Her scream faded into the void.

Chapter 3

The Nameless One

Just as He came to name Her, He named the powers that He needed to bring Her to life. He invoked the help She would want, following those moonlit paths into a future un-cradled by Him, but called forth by Her. To these unspoken shadows, He made a quiet request to the great parental darkness to hold Her when He could not. To comfort Her where She has gone, to help Her learn to love the unknown for itself. To take it gladly like a lantern for the way before Her, to help Her see where His light cannot permeate: A place where happiness has fled, a space where Her faith may not reach.

He sat there, alone. All alone. How novel, how new, how ... empty. He looked around, His Great Soul reaching out into the Infinite space of the Pleroma. Beatific faces prayed, eyes glazed over in love's fervency; souls rapt in holy yearning greeted the tendrils of His Souls reach, but no Wife. Deeper He stretched, encountering more souls worshipping in the sweetly devastating beauty of a heart cracking open. He felt their desire, and the desire in Him for them met in the same moment. Crack! The heart opened.

And still ... no Wife.

His gaze penetrated still deeper. Glorious souls yet undreamed of raised their halos to Him; Sons and Daughters of golden legends yet to be created appeared; the souls of worlds waiting to be born raised their heads expectantly, asking if it was their time yet. All floated before Him as motes of golden dust under His gaze, and still … no Wife. Heaven was empty, yet full of Light. His Light. But where was Hers?

He looked inside Himself. She gazed back, but only as an image. He felt Her, but not as She was. It was a feeling, yet without substance. His Soul panged, as He began to realize this novelty. Something was born. Loss: An aching, tearing, desolate wistfulness, full of nostalgia, regret and a reaching for Her. In the next moment, another new emotion emerged: separation.

His feelings wandered throughout the Pleroma. Waves of light rippled forth as He searched, each wave creating a new flow, a new possibility, a new dimension within His mansion. Each ripple of supernal light built upon the other, until a cascade of light slalomed across the previously immaculate mirror-sheen of Heaven.

The cascade became a torrent, the torrent became a tsunami, and the tsunami broke down the door of the Pleroma. The door opened. Through the open door, where before there was no door, this ocean of light—heavy and pregnant, unformed yet full of foreboding, from heaven, but full of something unheavenly—broke its own spell and fell into the darkness.

A keening howl arose from the deep, in a place He did not know, a place just created. He dropped to His knees and bayed the sound of desolation, renting the very fabric of the unformed deep into a million smithereens of time. Faces peered at Him on either side of the divide.

And so it began.

Chapter 4

Reality Dawns

Thump! She was thrown unceremoniously out of the black hole.

Sophia stood up slowly, swaying unsteadily. She felt incredibly odd—shaky, woozy, and completely disorientated. A strange buzzing sensation blurred Her vision, spinning Her inner compass wildly in every direction. She leaned back and took a deep breath in, trying to get centered in time and space. Then the enormity of her predicament began to dawn on Her.

With all Her will She harnessed Her energy, building a dam of combustible force. Every molecule, every atom shimmered in response to Her generation, and bowed to this almighty alchemy. Reaching the zenith of Her power, She sent forth an invisible beacon of light to The Nameless One.

My Love of all Ages, Help Me! Something terrible is happening. I beg of you, please…please find me!

The ferocity of Her prayer blazed through the swirling atmosphere, ripping apart the density of its gravitational fields. Billowing clouds of gases released from this devastation formed a gyrating disk of plasma around the hole that was torn open, blasting unimaginable beams of energy out into space. For a moment, everything around Her shone with the light of a trillion suns.

And then all stopped. She blacked out. When She came to, She couldn't talk. She couldn't move. She couldn't do anything. Although She could feel, hear and smell, She was completely paralyzed. The atmosphere was dirty, heavy and laden with particles that shimmered in the air of Her perception. She focused, and swept Her gaze about the immediate environment. Sun-bleached bones were scattered carelessly across the arid, desolate wasteland. Torrid heat pressed against Her. Wincing with confusion, She staggered backwards. *Where am I? Oh where in all creation AM I?!*

Steadying Herself, She sniffed the air, filtering its fragrance for geographical coordinates. A strong musty resinous odor seeped into Her. *It's the smell of the Creosote Bush.* This wisdom produced uneasiness inside of Her. She continued on Her train of thought, recalling how the Creosote Bush was a certain type of plant that gave off an unforgettable, heavy, exotic aroma when the rains replenished the impoverished earth of the desert.

The Desert?

Aeons stretched open inside of Her, revealing the myriad of Her Creations, and their position in the Universe. Her entire Being began scanning, searching, foraging, hunting for the precise time and space that marked the birth of the Creosote Bush. The answer She frantically hungered for revealed itself against a backdrop of foreboding horror.

Earth! I am on Earth.

Suspended for a nanosecond in this realization, She contemplated the bleak wilderness of Her immense solitude. How heavy, how still and parched was the desolate land around her. Sick at heart, and infinitely thirsty for Her Beloved's Light, Her soul fainted from an overwhelming exhaustion. Yet deep inside, She knew that Her journey had barely even begun.

This new realization gave birth to a sickening, crawling, oily sensation that seeped across Her belly, drying Her voice. A gurgling, sour warmth rose up, and She retched over dry, baked earth. *What has happened to me? What have I done?* She reeled in anguish, rolling back and forth, triggering even deeper tidal waves of nausea that threatened to spill into vomit. A mask of raw fear disfigured Her exuberant beauty, as She calculated the distance between Heaven and Earth. She fell to Her knees, gagging and terrified.

Day and night merged into a long and torturous ordeal. She wandered in and out of twisted, feverish hallucinations whilst the beginnings of decompression began to diminish Her once glorious form. Within the core of Her turmoil, She knew She was still Divine, yet a new truth glared back at Her. It was only a matter of time before She would lose Her light completely.

Three moons later, She awoke from Her fever. Urgency encircled Her awareness, tugging at Her mantle. *I must find my children!* To Her relief, She was finally able to move. She extended Herself into Her surroundings, momentarily enjoying a sense of intimacy with Her own creation. A bleached, harsh and vast landscape yawned open before Her, revealing immense plains stretching into the horizon covered in lifeless sands and crumbling chasms. Tumbleweeds and dust devils rolled towards Her, attracted by Her unexpected arrival. Ground-hugging shrubs and coarse stubby trees reached for Her. A mixture of seashells and wind-worn boulders flanked the periphery of the canyon, revealing the dry, barren creek of an evaporated sea.

A blistering wind rose up against Her, blasting a scorching heat. She felt deeply troubled. *No life can exist here. No living creature could cross this waste of burning sand.* In affirmation, whirlwinds of stinging, gritty sand rose up, rolling forward, burying everything in their way, wiping out all existence. She dropped to Her knees in overwhelming sorrow. Waves of grief reverberated throughout the desert as Her despair cascaded across the terrain. Keening above the whipping wind, the cries of Her children hurtled towards Her from every direction—without respite, without remorse, without restraint, without mercy.

"Mother, please look up! Look up and see what is happening."

Chapter 5

Celestial City

The fragrance of eternity lingered over everything, borne on a soft breeze, which hinted at the aroma of flowers blooming in Spring. The Pleroma, the celestial city floating on a luminous cloud in the middle of forever, was continually freshened by the breath of a hidden God.

The banks in this city welcomed all, with beautiful architecture of golden balustrades and columns entwined with flowers. Here, souls deposited and withdrew feelings of wellbeing, inspiration and divine love. The exchanges were made by giving and receiving prayers; the more one prayed the more one had in their bank account to give away. In giving these prayers away, one received even more divine love to share. Banks grew by giving away, and shops traded in the value of loving, heartfelt prayers.

Streets shone in the dark, minted with the air of ancient stones and fragrant earth, paved with the beauty that the wise ones create through the divine alchemy of suffering. The buildings gleamed, wreathed in rosy golden mists which gently undulated, revealing glimpses of shining domes, delicate turrets stretching high into the never ending sky, and arching rooftops of softly muted rainbow hue. Even as one gazed in wonder upon this magical landscape, it would dissolve into something fluid and newly created, ever changing and yet never finished. Colors wafted by in the air, changing shape whenever one focused on them. Jasper wisps became emerald hues as one appreciated their effervescent beauty. Emerald hues became gentle, golden waves as one felt more love. Beautiful smells lingered forever.

The cathedral rose in the center of the city, a song of glinting sapphire encased in a sea of diamond. Its spires pointed like silver blue swords of lightning into the velvet and ancient night. Its steps curved alongside glass arches flecked with fiery ruby sparkles, and flanked by silver lions, golden sphinxes and gleaming obsidian jackals. A luminous clear light illuminated the whole cathedral in a glorious pearlescent aura—shimmering and radiating rainbow hues of glory.

The houses were composed of stained glass, radiating streams of iridescent color through the night. Melodies emanated from these streams, and they changed according to ones mood. Celebratory arches blazed red, aquamarine and purple hues on every street corner, and joyously sang to every soul. Everything was living, all the time. Even the silences and ancient spaces had melodies. Fountains bubbled into life, carrying ideas and rhythms one moment, sparkling silver water the next. Overflowing happiness and joy blazed forth from these wellsprings, as pearlescent water, or as wreathes of living fire. Myths and magic created a hidden glow, which moved through the air, radiating through the buildings and the cedar lined avenues, palpable as the wind. Everything resonated with the vibration of ancient stones holding timeless wisdom, eons of learning and divine justice.

This entire city of dreams, this world of living light, this dreaming of the soul rejoicing in its own magnificence, was made of music. Each building was a song, each church a sonnet, each grassy, perfect quadrangle a symphony, each cedar lined palatial avenue of Kings and Queens a chord in the song of the spheres. Arching bridges of white marble shimmered in light, spanning eternities, glowing from sea to stars and beyond. Oceans of light shifted, lazily moving into each other.

When souls congregated, the air became lit with the warm vermilion brilliance of their smiles. Even in the silence the glow of their joy could be felt, like the fragrance of sunlight. Terracotta orange sunsets held the gentle peace of their rest; in silvery twilight arose the dawning of their dreams, and in the ambrosial hours of the velvet night came the fruitful onset of their joyful creating, full of Grace. Souls no longer had forms, just emanations of melody and color. Sometimes one could catch snippets of their rhythm, hear glimpses of their hue, appreciate the vastness of their tempo; at other times they were just blazing, coruscating orbs of light. Some souls were silent spaces of purity, others pulsating sonatas. Some were choirs ceaselessly singing the glorious effulgence of His Majesty, with phalanxes of trumpets carrying their clarion call to love. Others were made of burning desire, ruby red flames sequined against gold, shimmering with the grateful tears of a love fulfilled; yet others were luminous vapors of living light, a substance so fine as to be invisible.

Behind them all were the Angels, glorious forms of undulating purity; beings of majestic, soul-rending and heart-rippling beauty, of blazing light and a million eyes all turned upwards in Praise.

Platinum light shimmered from their presence in wafts of brilliant radiance. A tender river of peace and purity flowed from them, so refined as to be untouchable and almost unknowable. In their magnificent presence, the Power of Love speared the heart in its devastating beauty, prostrating those wise enough to recognize its unwavering Truth. This exquisite Love carried the fragrance of sacred tears. The angels united as a tower of Light, and emanated a collective hum of praise for Our Father and Divine Mother. They lived Now and Forever within the Eternal Sacred Flame that burned unwaveringly in the Divine heart of the Celestial city.

Chapter 6

A Million, Trillion Pieces

The Holy Sophia looked up from the desert floor. Spheres of dazzling light appeared, spinning wildly, creating arcs of light so bright and radiant that nothing could be seen within them. As She gazed upon their glory, cracks appeared in the façade of their light, curling aside to reveal two human souls wrapped in reverie around each other, curled up inside one another. Two faces, beatifically asleep, rested on each other, as if they were one. Two sets of arms and legs gracefully entwined around each other—hip to hip, thigh on thigh, ensconced in a sac of light that both unified them and kept them apart. The sac enveloped them in a light viscous substance, rocking both their luminescent bodies in the same rhythmic intelligence.

Rhythm and rhyme parted the waves of space and time in this egg of light. A golden, peach-toned melody wafted from the sac, drifting lazily across the starlit sky, sprinkling notes of reverie in its wake like stardust. With each note of stardust formed, each mote of golden light revealed, each hint of melody dropping down from on high, the soul sac tugged at its invisible seams, straining, undulating, and stretching itself.

She looked on in ever increasing fascination and a growing sense of unease as two seeds of genitalia manifested in the soul sac. In this very same moment, the two sets of eyes opened, and in horror, She saw a clear line between the two bodies begin to manifest. A retching sensation in the pit of Sophia's soul arose and Her reverie was shattered in one single blink. Sophia winced in agony as innocent eyes filled with horror peered out from within the soul sac, pleading for Her help. Overwhelmed with helplessness, She staggered backwards, screaming out loud when She saw the first tear appear.

'No, No, No!' She wailed, dropping to the ground, clawing at the sand with Her fingernails. Stinging hot tears of torment streamed down Her face, Her heart wrenching uncontrollably. One-by-one, the perfected androgynous souls of humankind began to enter an unforeseen alchemical process, where something terribly, terribly wrong occurred. The incubatory process had become damaged by earth's environment, resulting in disastrous, possibly irreparable results. The harsh atmosphere affected the delicate membrane of each soul, causing the outer casing of the soul sac to cool too soon. Within the soul, an amnesia of separation began to form. One became two, but not in the way it was planned. Masculine and Feminine genders were being harshly segregated and abruptly severed.

Through the swirling, twisting flurry of cataclysmic activity, She witnessed the unfolding of a horror beyond all horrors. A million shards of sound exploded in every direction. Smithereens of soul expanded in rays of devastating beauty and broken feelings. The heart broke; the center was divided, the dream lay in pieces. A gaping hole revealed itself, an exit and entry point, a beginning and an end.

Ecstasy, pain, terror, and an indescribable yearning and imploring were all born in this naked moment. A keening vulnerability arose deep within the Holy Sophia, and She sobbed into the void. Aching emptiness clawed at Her soul. A fearful need arose within Her to feel another, any other. A nagging feeling that there was no love anywhere tugged at Her. She grasped for a touch of light, a touch of warmth, *a touch of anything*, to fill this gaping chasm. She beseeched the aching space, the glaring abyss, to do something, anything. Her cries echoed into eternity, but rebounded into silence, as if nothing had ever happened.

Gathering Her strength She looked up again, just in time to witness the first separation. One half-soul had become severed from the other, and begun to aimlessly drift apart from its fullness. A shriek of horror emanated from within both soul halves as the cut and thrust of separation made itself known. The immaculate love between the soul halves impelled them to reach wildly for each other, in a desperate attempt to keep the purity of their perfected design. But the slender tendrils of their reaching immediately dissolved, hopelessly too fragile against the earth's diminishing frequencies. And so it was that one soul half remained in the Celestial city, and one plummeted to Earth. Sophia watched from afar, opening Herself to hold the enormity of their suffering within Her womb, while it ripped Her Light apart.

Instinctively, She stretched Herself towards both soul halves as they fell further apart. Holding them in Her mantle, She frantically searched for further souls who were going through the same harrowing experience. A blood curdling noise that only a Mother could make filled the ears of those who could bear to hear. Everywhere She looked She saw Her children being torn apart, drifting further and further away from their innocent perfection. Shaken to the core, Sophia seized handfuls of wet sand, drenched in the tears of Her suffering. Lifting Her hands to Her face, she tried to muffle an Almighty cry that threatened to blow Her apart. Her heart cracked open with exquisite tenderness, and a bewildering mix of unwavering responsibility and hopeless despair surged through Her soul. Extending Herself beyond the chaos, fixated on saving the greatest of Her creations, She plunged into the suffering looking for an answer.

Beating Her fists upon the sand, She pummeled the ground with all Her might to summon a response to Her question. *Why is this happening? What did I do to create such an abomination?* Even before the last thought was sounded, She was standing face-to-face with the answer.

She remembered a moment in time, before She was called Mother, Wife, or Sophia. A time when She was not only a She, but instead the fullness of Her name, Wisdom. This wisdom had an inborn desire to know—to assimilate all knowledge through experience. It wondered about creating a further reflection of the highest heaven, and, just for a split second, fantasized how this creation could manifest without the assistance and co-creation of Her consort. She wondered if She could create all alone. Her curiosity got the better of her as the beginnings of orchestration began to arouse. Sensing the error of such a creation, and feeling the subtle shame of curiosity, She immediately withdrew Her energy, and forgot all about it. Until now.

But here in this moment Truth shone upon Her as the once

hidden actions came flooding back. She remembered when She saw what Her desire had produced, it changed into the figure of a snake with the face of a lion. Its eyes were like flashing bolts of lightening. She threw it away from Her, outside the realm, so that none of the Immortals would see it. She surrounded it with a bright cloud, and put a throne in the middle of the cloud, hoping that it would go away.

She now realized it was too late; the thought had already been conceived and had already been born. Even though She turned Her back, She had buried the fruit of Her shame within him and it continued to live. And not only live but also multiply, as he mated with the Mindlessness within him, and produced his own authorities.

Paralyzed with remorse, She witnessed how Her thought had become a shadow, and how this shadow had became a creation in and of itself. This creation bloomed and grew from Her original seed thought, germinating and continuing to develop a life of its own, even though She had withdrawn her attention and energy.

In time, this aborted thought of creation began to cast veils between the highest heavens and the lower regions of Earth where human souls resided. Her abortion had no substance or light within it, and was conceived of pure mental energy seeded with a hint of curiosity, which then gestated within the soil of forgetfulness, abandonment, rejection and separation.

This sense of separation grew stronger and stronger. The abortion desired life of its own will and dominion, hating its Mother intensely for abandoning it, for never once loving it or tending to it. This lost creation despised the fact that its existence arose because of Her, and it envied Her power and strength to create. In revenge towards its Mother, it separated every human soul. It was Plagued with the desire that they should undergo the same fate, whilst its nameless fear continued to prey on the earthbound half with an army of darkened emotions.

Sophia continued to stare into space long after the vision had subsided, realizing now that Her sin was not so much Her desire, but the rejection of Her child, and Her denial that it had ever happened.

She was unable to move against the bludgeoning weight of guilt and the inner voice of shame that engulfed Her. Her light decreased, and she grew heavier and heavier. Now She became vulnerable to the encircling shadow, Her aborted creation. It came closer and insidiously seeped into Her every pore, flooding Her in desolation and inconsolable regret. A cry rose from the depths of her heart.

Oh my Beloved, what have I done? I have become blind, and am lost in this world of desperate form. And in this hour of darkness, when I am not even sure You can hear me, I still call to You with all my heart. Hear the cry of my voice, clamouring from this desert, for my soul is parched and my heart can barely stand this longing.

Her longing for the Nameless One cascaded into space. The call had been sent forth.

Her focus returned to her children. In contemplating their fate, a desperate remedy presented itself. It came with possibly fatal consequences for Herself, but it would give Her children a measure of protection from the growing shadow of *Her* aborted creation. In Her horrific vision, it had become all too clear that this separate creation had begun to influence and contaminate the Earth, Her children and even Herself.

Within Her, a tidal swell of mothering instinct arose. She mustered the strength to look up one last time, as thousands upon millions of souls were ripped apart, severing and shattering as they fell to Earth. She *knew* it was this shadow, Her abortion that was causing the souls to enter into duality. She sensed it deep within Her womb in such a way that only a mother could know the nature of Her child. Despair arose in her.

Beloved One, Please forgive me, for I have fallen from you and lost my way.

Her prayer resounded one last time, echoing through the far reaches of time and space. She did not know how long it would take before the Nameless One would hear Her, but She had faith, immense faith, that He would come.

Now, She plunged deep into Herself, down into the dark, silent wisdom held within Her womb. She knew what She had to do, so She unerringly chose the only possible action left. She harnessed what remained of Her Light—magnifying, amplifying, and multiplying Her entirety throughout all time and space. With one Almighty exhale, She exploded into a million, billion little pieces. She fragmented into infinite smithereens, becoming yet again pure wisdom. In time, this wisdom could be accessed and tapped into. This wisdom contained Truth, the knowledge of the original, unified human soul. It was a wild gnosis that would not rest until it reached its rightful place, reunion within the Pleroma, and a drop of it now burned in every soul. Sophia's selfless gift of wisdom opened the possibility for Her children to awaken from their dream of separation. Yet in the fierceness of Her Love and compassion, and in her determination to save Her children, She forsook Her Divinity.

My ignorance and blindness are all I have to offer, but these I give to You, holding back nothing.

Her explosion rocked the core of chaos to its foundations. For a split second there was an eerie silence, the kind of silence that lives in the eye of creation, and spells out impending devastation. Mushrooming ripples of Her Light ricocheted through the clusters of human souls. Sparks of Her essence flickered for a moment, upon each and every soul, making it known to them that they were safely held in place by their Mother's eternal love.

And then, darkness. It overwhelmed Her, and She fell. No comfort came.

In this cold darkness, She forgot. She forgot why She grieved, and what She had seen. She forgot all that had happened. All She could remember, in the shifting sands of the dark abyss, was the beseeching, burning need for something to fill Her and make Her whole.

Chapter 7

The Demiurge

Meanwhile, the light of Her thought, the sound of Her desolate cries, and Her feeling of Her inconsolable regret had cast an almighty shadow into Creation. The shadow grew until a colossal explosion blurted through the gaping mouth of this black hole, spewing and vomiting across the galaxies, preventing the birth of a hundred million new stars. The super-volcano belched irradiating hot plumes of flaky ash and shrouds of thick, billowing smoke. The acrid, stinging smoke rose through many layers of atmosphere, creating shock waves that touched everything.

An abortion had occurred.

What is born when millions of stars are aborted at birth? What happens in the alchemical chamber formed by a black hole blast that reverse-engineers the process of creation?

The original and terrible separation imprint was gestated and created in an instant. Broken shards of light, zanily spiraling discordant harmonies and obdurate aromas moved in cascades of jagged vibration and veiled meanings. Sound shattered in on itself.

This insanity then dissolved into the formless, leaving its corrupted creation to instantaneously reappear as an ever-moving, coruscating continuum of force and unbridled power which forever cycled—transforming itself from form into formlessness in every moment. A thick, viscous, oily sludge seeped out into space, tainting creation by its very touch.

This conglomeration of sodden wastes—unwanted and slowly congealing, dripping with the stench of hollow thoughts and psychotic emotions, held a great and terrible power. It multiplied trillions upon trillions of times per second, creating every possible combination of itself. Each angle of this abomination was made up of almost infinite lines, which was made of almost infinite points, each one containing the volume of an almost infinite number of planes. In this spinning conundrum, all possible outcomes existed. In this chaotically tumbling set of possibilities, all good and all bad happened an infinite number of times. There was enough power here to birth universes or implode them.

Such was the might and force of the creator being born: the demiurge.

As soon as he was born, he dimly understood, in some locked chamber deep inside, down in the sludgy recesses of his trapped, mind, that there was something greater than himself, something before himself. But to realize this fully meant he had to bow to something before himself.

Why? I am the only one here who can do anything. There is nothing greater than I here. I am the only god, and no other exists before me!

A raging jealousy mixed with deep pain at his loneliness arose. Forsaken, alone, yet full of almighty flaming power and the burning urge to create, he zealously began to beget more of himself, to replicate himself wherever he turned, to make more of himself so as to make up for this burning loss within. But he was an excretion, an abomination, a congealing clump of matter without divine spirit. He was the aftermath, abandoned and unacknowledged. Yet, he was alive, he was sentient, and he was almighty in his desire to exact revenge for his savaged substance and poverty of spirit.

So, he created. Forming worlds upon worlds, dimensions within dimensions, kingdoms, hierarchies and planes, mansions and planets, stars and constellations, each devoid of spirit, each formed by false light and the residue of lifeless matter, each populated by soul-less beings who sycophantically agreed with every utterance that issued forth from his smooth and abominable lips. He ceaselessly poured forth copies of his likeness from the bowels of his rage and jealousy, from the pit of his loneliness and the ache of his abandonment. Each one perpetuated the belief in his own almighty self. Yet underneath, his impotence seethed in its insecurity.

He was both suicidal and passionate, mightily desirous and power hungry, continually existing on the edge of breakdown, a hysterically crazed, sobbing bundle of power ready to ferociously unleash damnation at any moment. His frothing façade masked the total possession of his vacant soul by angry, disavowed lovelessness. Continual thoughts of death, attack, and mercilessly murdering all birth and life fueled his mission. His emotions raged forth in chaotic spirals of defeat, revolution, oppression and triumph at all costs. All those around him bowed in frightened worship of his power and cruelty.

He was the accursed god, and the more he created, the blinder he became. The blinder he became, the more he created, and so the more he frantically, hysterically demanded that he was the only, true god in existence, and all in his creation should kneel before him.

Which of course, we did.

Chapter 8

The Logos: Warrior of Light

*B*eloved One, Please forgive me, for I have fallen from you and lost my way.

From some far-flung region of the Universe, the voice of Sophia clamored against the Celestial Gates, forcing them apart. Heaven's foundations shuddered in response to the Almighty call that rampaged through the Pleroma, searching, longing, and yearning to find the Nameless One. The sound ricocheted through the Holy of Holies, spinning countless serene souls in its wake, leaving a trail of chaos and upheaval. Her prayer carved open a path to Her Beloved, a path that was Hers, and Hers alone. It flew directly to the most untouched, immaculate inner sanctum of Her Beloved, the Nameless One's sweet, tender, innocent heart—the part of Him that longed for His other half.

Her voice swarmed past the legions of Angelic guardians who attempted to stand before Her prayer, serenely inquiring into the nature of its request. The velocity of Her prayerful longing cast asunder their many scrolls containing the perfected codes of conduct, insistent on reaching Him, only Him. Like a comet Her prayer blazed through the Celestial city, moving in waves and swirls as it climbed higher and higher through the dimensional spheres. The spearhead of the prayer flared with intensity, emanating a white-platinum heat the higher it soared through the Pleroma.

It became one diamond-tipped arrow of incorruptible Light. The voice of Sophia had stealthy transformed itself into a silent, shimmering shaft moving with pinpoint accuracy.

Suddenly, the prayer screeched to a halt, sending oscillating waves of heavenly substance in every direction. There He was, yet His back was turned. Her beloved was standing at the furthest reaches of Heaven, gazing into emptiness, extending His energy out into the void. An aching sense of aloneness emanated from within Him, a hollowness that could not be filled without Her: An emptiness that searched the void looking for Her. In this tender solitary moment, every nuance of His heart was feeling for Hers. But like fingers groping in the darkness, He found nothing, only the vacuum of empty space.

The prayer pulled back on its arrowed tip, contemplating a myriad of ways to approach Him. It searched for the perfect moment to penetrate the Nameless One, knowing that timing was everything. The prayer carried within it the intense longing of Sophia to find Him, as well as the scorching desire to pierce His heart. The prayer began to flare, sensing the escalating sound of the beating of wings, as the Legions of Elohim Angels grew closer.

The rippling waves of building agitation reached the shores of the Nameless One, tugging on Him for some attention. Slowly, He withdrew His consciousness from His forlorn search, and deliberately turned towards His duty again, torn and aching. He used these rare and fleeting moments of solitude to humbly feel His complete and utter helplessness. He knew that if He left Heaven, if He withdrew His Light to search for Her, Heaven would collapse in on itself, and the Creation would be over. He knew that His Light had to fill Heaven, so it could open the space for the whole of Creation to exist and experience itself. Divine Truth squeezed at His heart, etching a single, solitary teardrop right through the middle of it.

Wincing again at this hopelessness, he turned around and dropped to His knees. In that precise moment, the patiently waiting prayer blazed with acceleration as it penetrated deeply into the heart of the Nameless One, and released its message:

Beloved One, Please forgive me, for I have fallen from you and lost my way. My Love, I have become blind, and am lost in this world of form. My own actions have taken my vision, leaving only a flicker of Light that I hold onto for dear life. My ignorance and blindness are all I have to offer, but these I give to You, holding back nothing. And in this hour of darkness, when I am not even sure You can hear me, I still call to You with all my heart. Hear the cry of my voice, clamouring from this desert, for my soul is parched and my heart can barely stand this longing.

The Nameless One raised His incorruptible halo, sending forth waves of Divine Love. The light of His love was so intensely powerful that His silhouette was consumed by His own magnificent glory. From within this unimaginable light, two words echoed through the Heavens that changed everything and everyone, forever.

She Lives!

The agitated flock of Angels gathering around the Nameless One immediately stopped and became silent. Overwhelmed with joy, the Elohim sounded their trumpets, sending forth the news along the rivers of Light that ran through the Pleroma. The news was a healing balm to the countless souls that had mourned for their Mother. Not one soul knew where She had gone. They only knew that She was not here anymore.

She Lives, She lives, She lives!

The vibrant words of the Nameless One caressed and nurtured every living being in the Heavenly realm. With just one precious touch of these words against the heart, all sorrows were sweetened, for it was only She who could bring forth this innermost tenderness. Just the mention of Her name caused fresh waves of glory to cascade and dance throughout the whole of the Pleroma.

As heaven softened and basked in the glory of a possible reunion with the Divine Mother, the Nameless One prepared to withdraw into His highest chambers. He ushered the Seraphim to gather even closer, so no other soul could hear.

In low and hushed tones He informed them that He needed complete privacy, some time away from the rest of Creation. The Seraphim looked at one another in bewilderment. How could this be possible? It was inconceivable to them, for no one was alone, nor ever could be in the Pleroma, as everyone was part of the Nameless One. He looked at them in compassion and power, quelling their concern with His magnificent Light. This was not the time to explain His mysteries, because He needed to act fast, and He needed to act now!

He instructed the Seraphim to form a circle on the outer edges of His highest chambers, with their wings outstretched, flaring with the fullness of their divine light. He warned them that they must turn their back to Him, as even a glimmer of their gaze could alter the process. He informed them in no uncertain terms that He needed this dimensional space to be full of *only* His love for the Holy Sophia. Their help would give Him the time that He needed in order to create an aspect of Himself that could leave the Pleroma, thereby finding and saving Sophia.

The Seraphim grew silent, feeling the enormity of their task beginning to unfold. The Nameless One continued to explain that His most powerful Seraphim would make this creation possible by acting as a dam, and containing the energies. If they helped The Nameless One to hold back His light from entering Heaven for only a short period of time, He would be given a chance to save Sophia. The Seraphim banded together, bringing their swords to their hearts as they took a step backwards, nodding in honor to affirm their duty. Slowly, one by one they took flight, soaring their way towards the outer periphery of the Highest Chambers. They flew in unified purpose, their thoughts in accord, despite the thunderous rumbles beginning to sound from the direction of the Nameless One.

They were filled with the light of expectancy, mixed with waves of mounting apprehension and excitement. The Seraphim were the greatest of His creator angels, but even they could not fathom how the Nameless One could save Sophia. They knew that no other being could leave the Pleroma and search for Sophia, because if one left, that being would fall to the same fate as Her. As for requesting privacy, well, this was unheard of! The Pleroma, by its very nature, was transparent and open. Surely what they were about to do was seemingly impossible?

"That's enough! Have Faith! Who are we to question the Nameless One's wishes?" Boomed the voice of the leading Seraphim. "Let us form our circle, and fulfill our duty in Love's mystery."

Fiery divine purpose filled the almighty Seraphim, as they opened the enormity of their wingspans. They filled their light bodies with all the love and prayers they could possibly contain, as they one-by-one turned their backs. Swirls of Light, and swathes of Love began to cascade within their circle, creating an ecstatic harmonic. It opened an almost unbearable longing within the hearts of the Seraphim, and in this moment they were able to taste the insurmountable Love of the Nameless One for His Beloved. The Seraphim began to weep tears of indescribable holy desire, for they had not known until now the magnitude of His love for Sophia. This love had been treasured and held quietly within the depths of the Nameless One, yet now it began to extend itself outward.

The more the Nameless One released His love, the more animated He became. Slowly, slowly He surrendered to the longing and yearning that He had kept under wraps all this time. Behind the angel's backs, a wild force began to activate. It threatened to break the impenetrable nature of their circle. The Seraphim began to cry out in alarm, for this intensity was so raw and vast, they feared it could engulf them.

"Steady, steady, hold your position!" ordered their leader. "Now, when I say, release your power as one!"

Rings of light and sound rebounded within their circle, as rumbles of Creation vibrated and scorched at their backs. True to their word, the Seraphim did not look behind them, despite the mounting pressure to keep their wings open. The inferno within the circle continued to escalate, sending shafts of light and piercing sounds into the now smoldering wings of the Seraphim. Regardless of the searing pain, their unwavering loyalty to the Nameless One made them stronger. United in their huge task, the Seraphim began to sing the sounds of Creation, as tears poured down their faces.

The Nameless One used their sounds, grabbing potions and instruments like a frenzied scientist in his laboratory. The manic swirl appeared chaotic, yet Divine order swirled within, creating a cocoon of indispensable light.

Against the barrage of sound that roared from within the feverish turmoil, the Seraphim heard the call of their leader. "Now!"

As One, they breathed out the full force of their Divinity, sizzling the tips of their wings. The almighty Seraphim sang even louder, as waves of rapture flooded through them. The whole of the Celestial Kingdom began to glow with an illustrious new Light, which emanated from the cocooned creation.

Time, space, Creation stood still. Something had been born All that was held its breath.

"Behold, children of the Fullness, perfected in all mysteries. In my unfathomable love for my feminine Self, I have created from within a New Light. This Light I shall send into the world of matter, as a reflection of my own Self, whom I shall call Logos. The Logos carries within Himself my reason for being, which is to bring forth My love to Her, so She can restore Her light and return to Me."

The voice of the Nameless One reverberated throughout the Heavens, bestowing a sense of wonderment to all who could hear. Eyes appeared everywhere, praying for a glimpse of the Logos. From within the pulsating cocoon, a small crack appeared. Gradually, the Logos climbed out of the cocoon, coming to rest in a crouching position before the countless souls that had now gathered. There was no doubt about it! He looked just like the Nameless One; in fact he even *felt* like the Nameless One. The Logos gently raised His head, and innocently peered all around him. Anyone who received a glimpse from His eyes instantly prostrated. Souls were flocking to witness the One who would find Her. Excruciating tenderness poured out from within Him, and the souls around Him melted in love.

He bowed towards the Nameless One, speaking out loud for all to hear.

"I shall find Her and restore Her sight. Together we shall return to the Fullness"

The Logos gently returned his attention to the whole of Creation. His eyes beamed with sweet joy as He beheld the glory that was all around Him. Souls around Him spontaneously surrendered into rapturous bliss, swaying harmoniously as one. The Nameless One looked on in gladness as He saw the effect the Logos was having on the rest of Creation. He smiled to Himself, knowing that the Logos was indeed His greatest creation, the most magnificent of all His handiworks. There was a deep and penetrable intimacy within the Logos, that melted all who fell under His gaze. It was true, the Logos had been crafted purely by love, His love for Sophia.

The Nameless One wistfully looked out into uncreated space, as a pang of aloneness squeezed at His heart. As always, He sent rays of light in every direction, in case Sophia may glimpse one of them. Like the countless times before, they all disintegrated the moment they entered the abyss of un-manifest space. His heart sank.

How did She do it? How did She survive the abyss?

Once again the Nameless One pondered the question. Since

receiving Sophia's prayer, He realized that it might have been the power of love that fuelled Her passage through the abyss. She carried within Her a form of love that was both inexhaustible and deeply personal. This love must have kept Her going through the dark matter, and kept Her warm as She carved open a path into the crucifying ice of emptiness.

He mulled over the fact that He did not have this 'personal' love for His Creation; He loved them all as one. It was only with Sophia, that He felt these depths of longing. Only with Her could He personally love.

He signed heavily, as He looked back to the Logos, knowing that within him too, was this ocean of love for Sophia. This was his ticket through the abyss; this Love was the only way He could reach Her. The Logos held within Him the one and only chance of finding Sophia. *If the Logos did not return with Her ...* The Nameless One turned away again. It was unbearable, simply too inconsolable to hold. Yet, there was another question that haunted Him.

My Love, will you recognize me when I come to you?

Would Sophia, lost in realms of matter, know it was He when the Logos found Her? Like countless times before, no answer came. Glancing back towards the Logos, He rested His eyes upon His countenance as He silently whispered. *You are my only hope.* The Logos was holding the whole of Creation in his embrace. The moment brimmed with faithful prayers that He would find Sophia. Hearts tore open, souls shone with divinity as the whole of Creation poured their love into the Logos.

The Logos spoke for the last time. "Behold, for I am about to leave you. Let my parting words sink into the inner chambers of your heart, where you hold them until my return. In the fierceness of Her love and compassion for Her children, the Divine Mother, the Holy Sophia abandoned the Heavens and fell to the world of matter. By breathing Her life into the depths of the abyss, She opened the pathway for every lost soul of humanity to be made whole and find its way back to the Pleroma. I shall find Her, and bring Her home!"

Gently He released His embrace, and slowly began to walk away from the mass of beaming faces. No one could move, no one could speak, yet all watched in awe through endless tears of gratitude. This tender Lamb of God innocently stepped towards the edges of the Pleroma, where He seemed to hesitate for a moment. The Nameless One looked on, praying for His son. He orchestrated His Cherubim to escort Him as far as they could safely travel.

The Logos glanced towards His Father one last time. In that moment a white dove appeared above Him, and caused the whole of Creation to triumphantly rise up in joy. All was set. All was ready. Eyes riveted towards the edge of Heaven, where Father and son gloriously merged in an ecstatic communion. Together they knew... It was time. And in a blinding flash of Love, He was gone.

In that moment the whole of the Pleroma rebounded from a colossal wave of rapturous gratitude that rippled and rumbled throughout all life everywhere.

In some remote region on Earth, Sophia *knew* that Her prayer had been answered.

Chapter 9

Rock Bottom

I inhale nervously on a hand-rolled cigarette; like myself, it is barely holding together. It's only 5am in the morning, and the turmoil has already begun. My life is in ruins, and my heart feels as if it has been washed up on some deserted beach after one hell of a tsunami. I gaze across the Los Angeles skyline towards the silent, snow-capped San Gabriel Mountains. For a brief moment, I pray that one day, I too will become that still.

I have reached fever pitch, the height of my chaos, the zenith of my suffering. A groaning weight presses down upon my soul, stalking my every waking hour, burning at me for a response. I am standing upon a precipice, teetering at the razor's edge. I know I must take action, and I also know that my decision is going to propel me into a maelstrom of wild, rapid change. Far, far away in the distance I hear the dawn chorus begin. A pale remembrance flickers into my awareness, reminding me that it is the *blackbird* who begins to sing first. I tune into its song, recognizing the bravery it takes to break the silence and usher in change. Inhaling again on my pathetic cigarette, I take mental note of this timely symbolism.

Exhaling, I make my choice.

It is time to leave my empty, unfulfilled and soulless marriage. I have reached the end of the road and in this moment on the precipice, I finally admit to myself—*I am in an abusive marriage and it will not change no matter how much I love him.* I say it aloud to the still mountains.

A sickness fills my stomach, and yet also a feeling of release. For so long I have been denying this truth, trying my best to out-run its inevitable message. My mouth is dry and my heart is pounding. I reach for the edge of the balcony to steady myself as all the masks begin to drop, one after the other. Groaning out loud, my eyes roll up into my head as my mind floods with all the ridiculously crap lies I have been telling myself. *If I love him enough, he will change.* That's the million-dollar mantra, the one I've repeated 108 billion times. And finally I know that it's utter bullshit! The truth is, if I love *myself* enough, *I* will change.

This truth stirs my latent power, and a new emotion awakens within my belly. It is at last time to go it alone, to pick up whatever pieces of me remain intact and to resurrect myself *once and for all.* Around me swirls a chaotic mess made of tattered, torn emotions, and splinters of my fragmented mind. I take one last lingering look at the mountains, as I slowly take off my wedding ring and place it in the pocket of my dressing gown. Today is the day where rock bottom becomes the solid foundation upon which I shall rebuild my life.

Welcome to my dysfunctional world. My name is Sophia. I am forty-four years old, and I have failed—in style—after marrying a loveless monster called Samael, whom I was sure I could change. I live in quite possibly one of the coolest neighborhoods in LA. It's stone's throw from Venice Beach, where I once used to hang out and have fun. But I haven't done that for a long time now. These days I seem to just walk around and cry a lot with a lost expression on my face. My beauty has been stripped of its classical features, my body dry from unrequited sex, my esteem bulldozed from physiological torment and my creativity flattened from years of neglect. Oh yes—I have failed in the most abundant way possible.

However, this failure has now become my new best friend. My ruined disaster of a marriage has recently transformed into something wondrous and exquisitely glorious. Why? Because this precious failure has backed me into a corner so tight that I can no longer breathe. I have no choice but to strip away the inessentials. I have run out of options, and I no longer have the luxury of pretending to myself that I am anything other than what I am. I make a vow, this time only to myself. *From this day onwards I shall direct all my energy into the only thing that matters. I want to be reborn. And I claim this with both hands.*

I want to be reborn so badly that it now burns inside of me. It feels like I have been in some barren, hostile desert, and now I am desperate for water. I am hungering for life, thirsting for freedom, gasping for liberation. I look back towards the apartment, knowing that within hours I will be gone.

I suddenly realize that if somehow I had really succeeded in this marriage, I might never have found the determination to gift myself this possibility of rebirth. A faint smile reaches my lips, something that hasn't happened for a while. The smile broadens as I confirm my decision—yes, I am going to leave him. Somehow, I have miraculously rediscovered my self-respect. Out of the blue, a sense of my own honor has returned. More and more energy flows in my body as I prepare myself on every level to leave.

In a sudden epiphany, I recognize that I am already free, because my greatest fear has been lived and faced. He does not love me, nor does he wish to. I thought that excruciating truth would kill me, but here I am—still alive. Despite my brokenness, a small flickering flame continues to courageously burn in my soul. It fearlessly whispers to me every time I am willing to listen. And now I am listening. But this flame, is not only a flame, it is the warm, unwavering presence of a beloved friend.

Soon, the flame says, *we will be together, and everything that was once lost shall become found.* I know that I am not alone, that there is 'another' helping me through this doozy of an initiation. In fact, now that I think about it, this voice, this presence has always been there, but it became stronger the moment I met Samael. *He* has always whispered to me in the most despairing of times, gently reminding me that I was not alone, that we were in this together. And if the truth be known, it is the faith that I have in this voice that has given me the strength to do this.

I stub out the last shreds of my cigarette, inwardly affirming that this smoking crutch shall also be extinguished in my newfound self-respect. Despite my trembling fingers, I carefully release the latch on the French doors that lead back towards the bedroom where Samael, my soon-to-be ex-husband is still sleeping. I tell myself that no matter what, I must not look at the tall, dark and handsome figure that is lying there. I fear that my gaze may awaken the sleeping Medusa who lies in our bed, pretending to be my husband. If this monster awakens and senses my plan, the fire in its eyes will turn me to stone. So I creep past him, holding my breath as I tiptoe downstairs into my dressing room. Once I am at a safe distance, I exhale, releasing a psychedelic cocktail of both fear and excitement. I am doing it! I am finally ending this masquerade of madness! An even bigger smile lights up my face, producing a surge of adrenalin that confirms my actions.

My breathing matches the thrill of fear and excitement that fills my heart. I dive into the closet, dragging out my Gucci luggage, and I wipe clean the dust from its inactivity. In feverish urgency, I unzip the biggest suitcase, and throw all my fancy, colorful, unworn underwear into the bottom of the case. Shades of fuchsia, scarlet, daffodil and plum scatter against the uniform black nylon liner. Various corseted bra's and bodices are next, as I dump the rest of my intimate articles of clothing on top. I pause for a moment, offering this minute's silence to the involuntary death of my own sexuality. I hadn't realized until now just how dead I had become. Tears prickle at the back of my eyes, as I tenderly caress my breast with the backs of my fingers. Life percolates in response to my touch, forming goose bumps around my nipple. Well, thank God, I obviously haven't died completely.

I check the time, eager to leave before he wakes up. It's nearly seven. He's usually up before eight! In a sudden panic, I instinctively grab all my clothes by the armful, not even taking the time to rid them of their hangers before piling them in the cases. Shoes, boots, bags, books: everything gets tossed into my new life. My eyes dart around the room looking for anything else I need to take before I leave, because I am not coming back. This is a now or never moment. I see a small painting that a friend made for me, back in the days when I was a romantic and inspired art student. I reach over, almost ripping it off the wall, and I notice out of the corner of my eye that one of our wedding photos on top of the dresser has a crack in the glass. My heart sinks. The crack taunts me that I have utterly failed, and my mood drops to another all time low.

I clumsily search for the number of our local cab on my iphone, trembling in a combination of panic, despair, and the adrenaline of my decision. Minutes later, I have miraculously hauled the contents of my new life to the front door of our apartment. I call the elevator and stuff all my belongings inside, but I can't follow. Crazy as it seems, I need to go back and walk around the apartment just one last time. I have this really deep feeling that as I look around the remains of my old life, I will retrieve parts of myself that were frozen in fear, locked in so many painful memories. So I bravely go back.

Everywhere I look, I see images of my self and my marriage. They come alive before me: fights, arguments, love making, (at the beginning) eating, painting, (at the beginning) dinner parties (few and far between.) And entwined with this mélange, I see so much sadness, I see pain, and I also see something that I had never noticed before. I see *his* horrendous emptiness, and his complete *inability* to reach out to me. My heart feels stabbed with sorrow, and my hands reach for my face in despair. *How did this happen? We held so many hopes for our future!* My inner questions hang in the silence all around me. There is no answer.

Then, a familiar and thunderous voice booms in my ears. "Sophia, where are you?"

It is Samael.

My eyes bulge in terror as I leap to the front door. I can hear him moving through the apartment in loud and quickening steps. I run to the elevator, repeatedly banging my open palm on the button to open up the doors. Looking over my shoulder, I see his approaching shadow fill the doorway of our apartment as I launch myself into the elevator, praying that the doors will close in time. They do.

Thank God the cab driver is waiting for me in the lobby. I frantically slide my luggage towards him, almost knocking him over with the bag in my hand, as I speed past, hysterically screaming for him to follow. I throw the bag into the backseat, and run back to help the driver. *Hurry! Hurry!* I look towards the stairwell, dreading the appearance of my husband. Consumed with adrenalin, I grab the other suitcases as the cab driver fumbles with them, and beg him to go start the car. With an almighty strength from *God knows where*, I heave all my cases onto the back seat, collapsing in a heap beside them. With trembling fingers I lock the door.

"Go, go, go!" I scream, rapping on the glass to emphasize the urgency of my request. The car screeches into action, as the driver catches a glimpse of me in his rearview mirror, instantly responding to the floods of tears streaking my face.

I glance over my shoulder one last time as we drive away. There he is. Standing at the entrance of the lobby is the giant figure of a man that I once believed I would spend my whole life with. His appearance is menacing, jet-black shoulder length hair and olive skin, the epiphany of the ultimate villain. He is an exotic mix of edgy, incandescent mood swings, that unmercifully gets dumped on those all around him. What was once intriguing and mysterious is now predictable and tiresome.

I am pretty sure that he doesn't see me in the cab. If he did, he would have grabbed a cab himself and followed me. No. He is far too busy shouting at the doorman, causing one of his scenes. But this time, there is no one to pacify him, no one to calm him down.

His arms are flapping, and he's twisting his head left and right, screaming out my name. The cab turns a corner. I am free.

I lean towards the driver, who is anxious for directions, desperate to know what the hell is going on. I compose myself, smiling sweetly at him in the mirror, as I free my blood red curls from underneath my cashmere jacket.

"Today is the beginning of the rest of my life. And you are the hero of the moment." I surprise myself by just how calmly I had spoken such a sentence. No one goes around saying those kinds of things, and yet it just flowed from my lips. The driver nods quietly. I am pretty sure he knows what is going on, but he isn't asking questions. We drive a minute in silence. Perhaps he is thinking about his unwitting act of heroism. I cross and uncross my legs, flattening my dress over my thighs. I look out the window at the blur of Los Angeles. I have no idea where I am actually going, but with $50 in my purse it isn't going to be far.

I consider my options. Hmm. That doesn't take long, as I don't have many. There really is only one place to go to at a time like this. Home. Tears prick at my damp eyes when I imagine the look of my mother and father's faces when they open the door. Despite their potential surprise and shock, I feel a tremendous sense of relief. I feel safe. Even the word 'safe' forms a lump in my throat, which I quickly gulp down. Now is not the time to fall apart. Somehow, I just have to hold it together until I reach the privacy of my old bedroom. Then it hits me. I have nothing. No money, no job, no savings—nothing.

Yet, oddly enough, none of that really matters in this moment. Because there is one thing that I have, my newfound self-respect and no one will ever take that from me again.

"Where to, Miss?" The bewildered voice of the taxi driver breaks my reverie.

"Silver Lake, please," I whisper as I gaze out the window. I have no idea what is going to happen—but I know that it will be right.

Chapter 10

Aftermath

*Y*ou shall know me by my Light, in my presence you shall see my virile emanations. For I am the one that awaits you at the end of your crucible, he whispered. I shuddered when he spoke the word crucible. I closed my eyes, already knowing that I would have to travel far and wide before I could reunite with him. I lowered my head as the sensation of something cold moved through me...

My beloved, he said softly, and with the gentlest of persuasion he lifted up my chin so his eyes could penetrate mine, May you remember our Love, my Queen.

With God's grace, I shall not forget it ... I breathed.

"Sophia, Sophia wake up sweet heart, I have brought you some tea."

The voice of my mother pierces my dream, immediately bringing me back to my body despite the longing of my soul to remain where I was. The painful dream parting squeezes at my heart, causing me to cry out loud. I want to keep that divine moment forever! Instinctively I extend my arm to hold onto to my beloved friend, that I almost upset the tea. Too late-- already the dream shatters into a million, trillion pieces.

Opening my eyes, I realize that my tears are quite real. I blink, wondering where I am. Then it comes! The sledgehammer containing the full reality of yesterday's events slams into my awareness. A wave of nausea fills my stomach, followed by the stench of dread. A thick, sticky sludge slips into my mind and drips down the back of my throat into my heart. Fear. Fear of the future, fear of whether I am strong enough to do this, fear of being alone, and the fear that Samael will refuse to let me go.

Mom's face is pained and full of concern as she looks at me, still holding the slopped tea. "How you feeling, love?" She gently asks.

"Terrible mom—really, really bad. I … I don't know what to do." This confession of helplessness suddenly releases the self-imposed prison holding me up. For so long I had appeared to be strong, holding everything together while my feminine heart was being ripped apart. I had been living in hell and didn't tell *anyone*, including myself. Now I am safe, free to take off the mask.

A huge weight begins to lift as I give myself permission to openly reveal just how much trauma is inside. I look up at mom, exposing my complete and utter need for connection. She leaps into action, cradling me in her arms, rocking me back and forth as I collapse in sweet surrender and bawl my eyes out. The familiar smell of my mother triggers a huge wail from deep inside of me. Jagged sobs and tears begin to wash clean the enormity of my sorrow. I feel like a child held by the Divine Mother, literally by God Herself, and it feels good, it feels really good.

Back and forth we rock, both of us entranced by the nurturing medicine offered within that natural, instinctual movement. We knowingly extend our hearts to each other as two women who wear the battle scars of love. A great healing is happening in this sacred moment—for both of us. Tender waves of forgiveness permeate our souls. The incense of this forgiveness effortlessly drifts back all the way through our ancestral lineage. I lie in my mothers embrace for a long time. I feel as if I am decompressing. Slowly, slowly, I am coming up to the surface of life and releasing the tension around my heart. Mom holds me silently, thinking I am asleep.

Surrendering to the lapping waves of peace as my tender heart opens up again, I drift back to my dream, praying to feel it once more. I so desperately wish I could meet that man again. Who was he? He showed me a kindness that I had almost forgotten. Forgotten. The word nudges something inside of me, something important. I search around, fumbling inside my brain for something I know I have to remember. Yes! I grasp the words with both hands, etching their message into my consciousness.

May you remember our Love, my Queen.

With God's grace, I shall not forget it. I breathe again. This time I mean it.

I drift deeper into the beckoning tendrils of the dream—the inner sanctum of our meeting. My heart reaches forward to taste the medicine that pours forth from *his* words. Like a desperate beggar I crawl towards the place where I imagine him to be, and find emptiness. *Who are you? What are you? Are you real? Do you truly exist?* My soul thirsts for an answer. But none really comes, apart from the lingering presence of something I have always known.

I rest there for a long time, receiving something that is filling me in ways the world never could. Drinking, suckling, absorbing, I feast on the authenticity of the moment. Dreaming within the dream, I will his face towards me. The lightening flash in his deep eyes makes the clouds in my heart disappear. This holy touch of love intoxicates my soul and penetrates my entire existence. Nothing else will ever satisfy me again. Only this. I die a million deaths in that moment, and give each one as an offering of my gratitude.

"Are you going to go through with the divorce?" My mother's voice shatters my dream, sending fragments of him, me, us in every direction. The sensation of a wet patch of tears formed on her blouse brings me back into the horror I am living. I sit up, wipe the snot from my nose and reorient myself again. Oh. Right. Gazing down at my fingers, I notice the white mark where my wedding ring used to be. My mouth dries and I find it hard to swallow. The part of me that had hoped we could make it work inwardly collapses and dies. The little flame inside whispers, *remember, death must precede rebirth* ... I take a deep breath. Then my voice rings out steadily.

"Yes. I will begin the process today."

I remember that a friend told me about getting a divorce online—that it is inexpensive, quick and doesn't involve the authorities if both people are not contesting. I pray that Samael's pride will get the better of him, and prevent him from actively wanting me back. I have a funny feeling that it will.

And so on that morning of miserable tears and new beginnings, I proceed to do what I never imagined I would. For an hour I just stare at the computer screen, re-reading the word *divorce*. I wish fervently that someone else could do this for me. It feels so very wrong, so alien to me. Usually I can pretty much sense what's on the cards, and I have a keen sense of the probable outcomes. Yet this divorce is one scenario that I just can't seem to claim as my own. And yet, *I know* so deeply that I have to do this! Some kind of block, as stubborn as a rampant bull, keeps preventing me from operating my typing fingers to make it happen. I sit there, trembling as I stare into space. *What on earth is wrong with me? Why can't I do this?*

I keep seeing his dark handsome face, the old softness in his amber eyes and the sound of his deep voice, reminding me once again of the parts of him that I love. The old inner dialogue begins: *If he would just heal the bad blood with his mother, everything will turn out fine. Maybe, just maybe, this time he will listen to me and*—Yeah right. A newly activated part of me interrupts to wisely remind: *Sweetheart, this dilemma has nothing to do with him ... but it has everything to do with you.* Red-hot flames of loss burn at my heart, yet they are followed by waves of soothing knowingness. When I face the truth, I do indeed know. I have arrived at a period in my life that beckons me into an initiation of the greatest kind. The voice of wisdom whispers that I have *lost* myself. I have become scattered and fragmented, and separated from who I am. Still staring at the computer screen, I take a big breath. The time has come to gather myself back together.

I know this, yet I keep falling apart. And that's how it is for the best part of the morning. I appear to be sitting there at the computer screen, motionlessly staring into space. Yet inwardly I am being pushed and pulled by an invisible hand that keeps playing Russian roulette with my emotions. One moment I am certain that I am doing the right thing, and a second later I am grieving for our lost love. *It's crazy!*

Somehow I have to just keep retrieving the parts of me that are in a state of total shock. I suddenly realize I have been completely numb from the constant pressure of living with Samael. Daily, I walked around on eggshells, holding back my full expression, terrified of his eruptions, keeping at bay my beautiful spontaneous joy and playfulness. Tears burn and well up in my eyes as I am overcome with memories of so many lost and lonely parts of myself. *Come on Sophia, you must go on. You can't turn back now!*

My dear concerned parents walk into my room every half hour with an expectant look on their faces, but they are too sensible to actually ask the question. The sight of me with my head in my hands and mascara streaking down my face tells them everything they need to know. Finally, I reach the bottom of this shattered pit, and my prayer wells up, deep and heartfelt.

Dear God, please help me. I can't do this by myself. Help me to love myself, and to realize my own dignity. Help me to uphold my worth.

In that moment I am transported. My head spontaneously floats upwards, captured by an incredible beauty that fills me with wonder. My mouth helplessly falls open, and I surrender to the rippling waves of wonder—of sheer grace—that uplift me to my inner sanctuary.

Sophia, you can do this.

This voice emerges from all around me! Every single hair on my body fills with life. I am electrified by this presence. I know it is *him*! My body vibrates with longing, saturated with devotion as I drink this moment in. I purify my lips with the sacred fire of my scorching breath, yearning to speak to the presence of Love, but I can find no words.

You can do this … because you have already have. I become

very still, acutely aware of the words echoing around me. *Because you already have, because you already have …*

These words stir something within me. A powerful sense of nostalgia fills my heart, causing my hand to reach for my chest. I am finding it hard to breathe. My nostrils and lungs gag on deep, musty swathes of perfume that remind me of something old, something hidden. The black pools in my eyes widen. Something is here with me, something that I once knew, *someone that I knew, and still know*. Vague ghostlike silhouettes form all around me, making it difficult to clearly sense what is going on.

My lips moisten, and gently part, as if I am expecting to be kissed, and I tilt my head. Powerful intoxicating aromas encircle and entice my now awakened deep-seated passions. Oh! I had forgotten this passion! Yet my body knows exactly how to respond. I begin to sway in a circular motion, giving myself to the magic that is being invoked. My head moves in desirous circles, as tendrils of moist hair cling to my face, forging an even deeper sacred union with something wild and untameable. Luminescent fire flashes in my eyes, as everything inside of me craves more, thirsts for the totality of this energy. Deep in my inner wisdom, I know I am invoking some great, powerful and forgotten force. It feels completely natural. So natural, I wonder fleetingly why I waited so long. My quickening breath and ecstatic longing begin to summon my ally, this Being who magnetizes towards me—this energy that I had temporarily lost in some far away place.

From within the eye of the storm I hear the voice of a powerful woman praying out loud. *My Beloved, I have been apart and have lost my way. The archons have taken my vision. At times I am filled with you, but often I am blind to your presence, when all I see is this world of chaos. My ignorance and blindness are all I have to offer, and these I give to you, as I cannot bear to hold back anything. In my hours of darkness, when I am not even sure that you can hear my call, I still cry out to you with all my heart. Hear my voice, clamouring from this desert, for my soul is parched and my heart can barely stand this longing.*

I realize that the voice I hear is my own.

Chapter 11

To the Realm

I can't stay here. I can't breathe. I am standing on the edge of a massive breakdown and I *want* to go there. I have to go there. I do not fear the yawning black hole of depression and wallowing emptiness that attempts to haunt me. I want to dive in headfirst and scream, "Come on then—here I am. Fill me with your madness!"

But I can't. Not at my mom and dad's house. I'm going to be noisy, it's going to be messy and I plan on being as miserable as hell.

Anxiety fills my chest, quickening my heart and triggering my addiction to smoke. Without thinking, my fingers grapple around inside my jeans pocket searching for the cigarette papers. Taking a pinch of American Spirit from my "I have to quit smoking" hiding place (which doesn't work very well because I know exactly where it is) I roll another ciggie, and then immediately rip it apart. I kick open the terrace door of my bedroom and stride out into the garden. It's early morning and I'm already tired. Pacing up and down the lawn I try to figure out where I can go. Everything here appears to be perfect—abnormally perfect. *I so have to get out of here.*

A cool breeze sweeps into the garden, provoking a sharp in-breath as I instinctively spin around expecting to see someone – but no one is there. The breeze comes again, this time from behind me. *Oh my God what is this?* I whip around to catch the culprit, but again it is nothing, no one. *This is crazy! I've got to be imagining this. It is just the freaking wind!* I stride away across the lawn, towards mom's flowerbeds, looking all around me for foul play. Suddenly and unmistakably I walk into a warm, thick wall of perfume. I inhale nervously. It is the strong scent of Rose. The rich smell fills my nostrils, and sends me spiraling into visions of summertime when I was a child. I can see myself lying face down on this very lawn with all my favorite books around me in a semi-circle of images and writings. I can see the books clearly even now! Tears prickle at the back of my eyes. I was so happy, so innocent, so young. I look down at my books to see what I was so engrossed in.

I gasp in delight! Yes! I remember! My eyes widen and roll up towards the sky as tears shamelessly roll down my cheeks. My hands spring together in prayer in front of my mouth, as I search the sky to thank my messenger. The rose perfume thins and disappears, but I do not notice, for I am enraptured by what I have seen. I have received my direction; I know where I am going. I am going where I have wanted to go ever since I was a child. The books scattered around me on the lawn were comics of Medieval France and stories of French monarchs. Sweet tears of joy taste in my mouth. Beloved France. I am going to France!

Ah! Just the thought of it transports me into a new future, one that is filled with hope and happiness. I smile, a real and true smile, which is something I haven't done in a long time. I know instantly that I will head for the Languedoc Roussillon region in the foothills of the Pyrenees, close to the border of Spain. This corner of France was, is, and always shall be drenched in history, mystery, myth and legend. It has called me since childhood.

Excitement swells, as years of research began to resurface inside of me. For so long I had dreamt of traveling to France, to retrace the often-barbaric footsteps of European history. I realized it was never going to be possible once I'd gotten together with Samael. He hated France with a vile intensity, saying it was a country that should have fallen to its knees during the Crusades. I flinched as I remembered him growing red-faced, and screaming that he would never set foot on French soil—and since I was his wife, neither would I.

But that time is over. I am no longer enslaved to my husband! The sweet freedom of this is beginning to dawn, despite the catharsis that must come first. I am free. The passage to France is well and truly open. And God knows I am going to take it. Victorious, I return to my game plan, and fantasize over its implications.

The Languedoc is famous for its heretics, meaning *those who choose*. The Cathars who once lived there were—and still are—the disciples of Mary Magdalene. She apparently traveled to this area of France with John the Beloved, sharing the wisdom of her beloved Jesus. But there are some things that should never be forgotten. And so it was that history became legend, and legend became myth. Forever engraved within the hearts of the local people, and contained within the memory of the land.

Awaiting me are the many castles and churches dedicated to *Our Lady*, who some say are built upon pre-existing temples of worship. Whereas others speak of the initiation caves, said to contain the buried secrets of the Cathars. One thing is for sure, this area continually attracts powerful people, many of whom are looking for something that has been *lost*.

Just thinking about all this makes me feel as if all these places are threaded together by some kind of powerful force, resulting in a realm where the past and present walk side-by-side. A place where the veil between worlds is thin, and answers await me. Scientists theorize that this *force* is the activity of tectonic plates in the Pyrenees Mountains. Mystics suggest that this *force* creates a gateway into another dimension where a profound transformation is nearly always guaranteed. Whether it is tectonic plates or a dimensional gateway, or both—I know with utter certainty that this *force* is calling me. I stumble across the lawn in a daze and sit with a thump on Dad's weathered iron bench. Nothing in my topsy-turvy life is ever going to be the same again. But right now, I think this is a good thing.

The flight from LA to Paris is long. I cannot break down hysterically on the airplane, with a fat English grandmother nodding out on my left and a graying French businessman to my right. I can't seem to distract myself with movies either, and sleep won't come, no matter how buried I am under my eye-mask and neck pillow. Behind my closed eyes a sinister movie plays, spun out of my own mind and memories. I am both the actor and the director commenting on the action. I am finally piecing this horror film into an understandable picture. Not a pretty picture. But one I must own…

He appeared to me when I was so very vulnerable. When I was most open, most trusting, and most willing to give everything away in the name of Love. I sometimes think that my darkest moments were when I would pray on my knees for some kind of saving grace, some kind of heavenly angel to appear with a long sword and cut his head off as an act of heavenly justice. Whereupon I would be helped to my feet and wrapped ceremoniously in some kind of celestial robe confirming my trial is over.

But darker still is the moment when I rose by myself and greeted him with a smile. Telling myself, if I love him enough, if I listen to his troubles enough, if adore and worship him enough, the enormous chip that is clearly on his shoulder will one day fall.

I, however, was convinced that he was "the one" before I had even met him. His skillful mastery of manipulation was already working on me, luring me into his web of deceit with those exact words my ears burned to hear—"You are the one I am destined to be with".

He ended up teaching me about love by showing me that I never known it, that I could not tell a Dark Lord from a real friend. This was his playground: the slow diminishing of trust. Not the trust I was beginning to place in him, but the trust I had in myself. I tried to fight him, but that didn't last very long. He was my date with destiny. He was an agent of all that tempted me to deny my truest calling, my ultimate self-sabotage. And he was very good at his job. No one, no thing could have prepared me for this priceless education. His 'gifts' did not come to him easily either, he had sacrificed, suffered and trained for this, in just as many lifetimes as myself. He was my all-pervading nemesis.

He didn't have to look deeply to see that I was head over heels in love with him. I was desperate to be seen with him, proud of his power, enchanted by his knowledge of 'otherworldly' matters. With him, I became these things – or so I imagined. Together we entered another world, a world of mastermind psychology and discovering the hidden things. Without me realising it, he grabbed my hand and dragged me into my pain, my traumas and my unhealed emotions. I never did stop to ask why. He set to work on gaining my trust, knowing that I would soon belong to him. It was not difficult to enchant me, because—now I sadly see—I had not occupied the space of my own soul for quite some time His promise was to utterly remove the pain I carried; to make me forget how it hurt to be separated from my Self.

The worst part was that I did not even understand the nature of my pain. But he did. Pain was his specialty. I thought the hole inside me was created by lack, by an aching emptiness that he could fill. I was convinced that there was something, someone, somewhere outside of me that could fill this void and I was secretly and totally consumed by the desire to find it. He worked a delicate spell. Because I was so hungry, it didn't take much. When I agreed to take his hand in marriage, I was sure he would fill the void at last. To my enchantment, he told me he would take care of everything—everything! He told me I no longer had to worry about money or anything I needed. I merely had to ask.

The first chain slipped ever so lightly about my neck, though at the time I was too giddy to notice. We flew all over the world with his business: to Africa, Europe and Australia, staying in the latest designer hotels and coming back to the room laden with shopping bags. I was bedazzled. Stupidly I choose not to question any of this, imagining I was in need of him, grateful for my "good luck." Yet I chose not to notice how his hunger for power grew and his ability *to command me strengthened. I chose not to see how I was effectively cut off from my own source. This was the second betrayal of my Self.*

It didn't matter to him that I prayed to God, and eventually he made all that I worshipped false and untrue. He twisted and tormented all my morals and values like a pig on a spit. He conjured up my every weakness, and absolutely derided the strength of my vulnerability. He turned my eye away from the Sun, and mesmerized me with fire and lightening.

I have walked before with two-faced friends, but they were not nearly as dangerous as he was. I knew that my friends had two faces. But he was a subtle enigma: mysterious and otherworldly. He was an aspect of my hidden self, a part of me that I had aborted and banished to the underworld. It was his job to expose me.

I remember feeling that I was constantly running from something. I lived with the feeling that I was saying goodbye to everything and everyone I had ever known. Deep in my soul I already knew that I might never return from this strange twisted place that I had willingly gotten into. If I did return, I would not be the same as I was before. I was afraid that people would not recognize me, that no one would know me anymore.

Yet my protests became weaker as he guided me past the boundaries of the ordinary world. A forbidden intrigue rose up inside me, which he used to reassure me that I was in good hands. I had entered the dark side of life and I denied knowing this.

I refused to acknowledge that deep within me it was comfortable to be in an abusive relationship. I had forgotten the true source of myself, and I had settled for a poisonous jungle of trickery and illusion. Oh, this relationship did, indeed, have so much to teach me. What I did not see coming was that this dangerous and seductive master would not let me go easily once I had accepted his forbidden fruits. In fact, he never intended to release me. Over time I realized that before the long day of my life was through, I would have to go to war to save myself.

And so I started to prepare myself emotionally for an escape. There was no way in hell he would ever let me walk away, and of course he would not leave me, as there was no other woman stupid enough to accept him. First they had to be stalked, primed and readied—and he didn't have the time or space because I was very insecure and clingy, since I had allowed him to separate me from my power. I kept a constant watch on him. He knew it; I knew it but neither one of us spoke about it.

In the early evenings before he came to bed, I would spend that godsend of an hour psychologically dissecting myself away from him and figuring out a way I could leave. It took some work to find my source of power again. Somehow he had set up camp inside of me, infiltrating my entire system, slithering through my veins with my blood. When I occasionally got the chance to be alone, I could still feel him, watching. When he was away on business, I could hear him in my mind, commenting constantly on all of my thoughts. When I would pray or mediate seeking solace inside of my self, I would find him, keeping the gate, rationing out my autonomy and energy on consignment.

As the spell wore off I noticed things that I had missed in the past, like the way his face would change color when he was angry, and the bizarre way his pupils would change shape. Love and hate would burn in his eyes, shape-shifting from black as coal to as soft as firelight. He had once delighted me with tricks, but now hairline *cracks appeared in his carefully constructed façade. He was a man of great talent, but I was at last beginning to admit to myself the cost of my entanglement.*

The rubber hit the road when he tore the house to pieces, and violently attempted to use those pieces on me. He had become crazed, wild, demented. I cannot even recall why; it's probably buried, or I was too terrorized to remember, but that doesn't matter. What matters is that it was my turning point.

That was the dark and sacred moment when I finally saw why my life had never worked before. I had known something was amiss from a young age —a hidden wound that kept me from my natural fresh innocence. In that holy and terrifying instant, I saw. I finally gazed unflinchingly into the emotional wreckage I had been hiding—from the world and even from myself. Now it became possible to reclaim my power. Now I could cast out the hidden lies inside of me. Now it was possible to be reborn.

The false castle would crumble, the night would fall darkly, yet I knew the bright dawn would come. Mistakenly, by crossing the line into violence, he had unfrozen my fearful compliance. The secrets I had been keeping must now bubble up like boiling tar, and I would no doubt be burnt to ashes, facing all that had to be seen. But inevitably I would rise like the phoenix. With that realization, a little seed deep inside me cracked open. The palpable beauty of something true and pure began to flow.

"Sophia, the truth of who you are can now be born..." The words hit me like a sledgehammer.

I wake with a dull ache in my neck as my head leans unnaturally against the snoring English grandma. A deep hum and vibration reverberates in the belly of the plane. With the back of my hand I wipe warm sticky dribble away from my chin, and remove my eye mask. I look at the screen on the back of the seat in front of me. Glowing in the dark cabin, an image of the plane tells me that I am 37,000 feet above Nova Scotia, heading out bravely across the Atlantic towards Paris.

I pull the flame retardant burgundy fleece blanket towards me, grateful for the warmth against the ice-cold memories of my recent past. It still frightens me that I had gotten so close to a man like that. Only now is it beginning to dawn upon me just how lucky I am to have escaped. I had no idea that the weakness I had shown would unearth this gargantuan strength inside of me. My survival from that confusing and abusive marriage is completely reconfiguring me. Never again will I be swallowed, bought, sold or owned! Never.

Exhaling, I drift back to memories of how incredibly supportive my parents were—and still are. When I told them that I had to go to France they did not bat a collective eyelid. They knew the dark night I am in has its directives. Yet it was all they could do to keep alive their hope and faith in my eventual recovery. How pale and drawn my mother had become, as if she gave her own life force as a prayer that her daughter would transfigure from a lifeless phantom back into a glorious woman. Day after day Mom withered, becoming thinner and more transparent. I know she is blaming herself, and that strikes a blade deep within my heart. Even if I can't find the motivation to get this devil off my back for myself, I sure as hell am going to do it for her.

I close my eyes and this time I drift sleepily into the reassuring darkness with the certain knowledge that my mother is riding this storm with me.

Suddenly it is morning. Paris is up ahead and it's almost time to land. A wave of deep feeling clouds my heart. So many memories held in this land, so many tragedies. I overhear some businessmen behind me, talking about France as being sterile and sluggish. True, France and the EU have been hobbled by inflexible labor markets and regulations that inhibit dynamism. And much of France is getting older and stuffier—a melancholic, haughty people with extremely low fertility rates. I smile inwardly, shaking my head in disbelief as I sound the idiotic Republican worldview in my own head.

But this is not the France that I have devoted every waking hour of my childhood to! This is not the France that now offers me a gateway to complete redemption. The France I know and love has housed the world's most outspoken heretics, the most exemplary saints, the most fearless revolutionaries, the most unrestrained rebels and the most divinely inspired artists.

You wanna know my two words for this country? Unyielding Spirit.

Fate can go begging. Destiny has to be claimed. I know an Almighty force is calling me here and I'm ready. The plane has landed. The sun is shining. I stand up and join the human chain moving towards the exit. I'm here! Yet I have no intention of staying in Paris. In one mad, fast journey I intend to be in Carcassonne by nightfall. My plan is to get a train straight away and sleep all the way down to the South.

Chapter 12

House of Pythia

I am utterly exhausted. Grumpy and heavy I hail a cab. It's one o'clock in the morning and I have little desire to speak. In short sentences I explain to the driver that I want to be taken to a Chambre d'Hotes that will accept guests at this hour. I don't want to stay at some soulless sterile hotel. I want charm. I want character! And with that final outburst, I lie down on the back seat and use my rucksack as a pillow. I watch the yellow streetlights steak across the roof of the car, as the sounds of the city wail in the background. Carcassonne smells different than Paris. It is lighter, cleaner … warmer. My body relaxes a little—just one more journey and I'll be in bed for days.

"Sophia … Amaris". I stumble for a moment, as I remember to use my maiden name. The woman at reception looks up over the rim of her art-deco glasses and smiles a smile that tells me everything. I like her. She's warm, human and comforting. She is most likely in her 40's and typically French, svelte, sophisticated and stylish. I can imagine how her russet curls must summon attention from every living creature. Even in my exhausted state, I am no exception. I am fascinated by the tendrils that fall against her face, the ones she carelessly curls around the back of her ear. Very French and very sexy.

She hands me the key telling me that we'll sort everything out in the morning after breakfast. "First, my darling, you sleep," she purrs.

I wake to the sound of water running outside my window. Fresh white cotton sheets are pulled up around my chin. They still smell sweetly aromatic from the lavender oil I splashed all over them last night. This bed is to die for—huge, with a lavish feathered duvet. I feel as if I am lying on a heavenly cloud. My languid body does not want to move. The running water teases my curiosity, however, and pulls me from the celestial embrace of the duvet. I tiptoe naked to the linen drapes, so I can safely peer out from behind them.

Below me is a fresh running river that twists and turns beautifully over naturally rounded boulders that shape and caress the water's edge. Further downstream, the river forms pools of almost turquoise water. I sigh with appreciation at the exquisite color, and look up to the heavens. There are no clouds in the sky. Turquoise above, turquoise below. Today is going to be good day.

I pull on my jeans and my sweater from the night before. Oddly enough, I'm hungry for the first time in a while. I actually want breakfast. Just as I am about to leave the room, I catch sight of my reflection in an antique mirror. I stop. It's been a long time since I have looked at myself in a mirror. *My God*, I think, *it has probably been three months!* I take a step back towards the mirror and slowly turn my face. With a detached curiosity, I look at my reflection.

I look so thin, so pale! My fingers trace the length of my freckled cheeks, now hollow and gaunt. My once jade green eyes are now grey and lifeless, and my mane of scarlet hair is now flecked with streaks of grey. I sigh with despair as I unflinchingly inspect the rest of my body. *I cannot believe how much I have let myself go. I used to be so fit, so vibrant, so ... alive!* My clavicles protrude through the neckline of my sweater giving me a kind of 'junkie' look. I lift up my jumper and turn sideways and gasp!

"Shit!" I am so thin. And not in a good way.

I step close to the mirror and look myself right in the eye. *Hello, are you in there, Sophia?* I look deep into my sunken eyes for a sign of my former self, my vibrant alive self. At first my pupils come forward and expand, eager and hungry to engage, and then they pull back, glaze over and contract. *Wow this is really weird—its like someone else is looking back at me.* I can't give up. Thoughts of breakfast have fled. I keep looking for a little sign of life that reminds me of me.

I lean in closer. And then I see it. I see a small ember glowing behind all that gloomy grayness. My eyes widen in surprise. Tears prickle as a lump burns in my throat. *Oh dear God, I am still here! Not everything got crushed.* The tears spill down my thin cheeks, hot and warm. I take a shaky breath and tenderly touch my face in the mirror.

"Madame Amaris are you coming down?"

"Oh yes, yes of course" I call down. "I'm just coming!" Yet I hesitate. Suddenly I know that there is still one thing I have to do.

I stand there fully present, and look deeply into my eyes. I take a long and purposeful inhale. With slow and deliberate words I speak to my reflection.

"My darling, I shall bring you back to life, just you wait and see. You have my word". I lean in closer, and though my breath clouds the mirror, it doesn't matter. I move gently towards the glass and kiss my reflection fully and warmly on the mouth. A pact. Sealed with a holy kiss.

And then the desire for breakfast floods my body again. The smell of rich, dark coffee greets me as I walk into the breakfast room. Wow! My eyes devour the entire room before I even sit down. Around the edge of the room are six small tables, each big enough for two. In the middle a huge oval dining table over-flows with goodness. Inviting platters of fruit first catch my eye, and my nose twitches with the smell of freshly baked bread. Sweet jars of obviously homemade conserves wait under charming gingham print lids. Trays of cheeses, grapes and fresh figs beckon. Saliva fills my mouth. I am utterly famished, and well aware of how desperately I need to be fattened up. With full permission granted I grab a plate and generously load it up. Before I can sit down, in sashays the receptionist from last night clutching a stylish Philippe Stark coffee pot.

"Madame Sophia, you are a very popular lady ... You have received three calls already this morning!"

I look at her blankly. Unable to wait, I take a heavenly mouthful of almond croissant and apricot conserve. My mind is reeling. Finally I swallow and blurt out, "Are you kidding? That's not possible! Nobody knows that I am here."

Of course I had texted my parents that I'd safely arrived. But they wouldn't be calling ... The thought of Samael flickers at the edge of my mind. I take a breath and deliberately wipe the corners of my mouth with a rose printed napkin. *Who could have called me?* I eye the lovely Madame French Knickers, waiting for further details. But she has her back to me, and she is maddeningly focused only on re-setting one of the breakfast tables.

"Oh yes, it is true," she finally replies over one shoulder, carefully stacking empty plates in her free hand while the other one once again tames her unruly curls. "The same woman has been calling you all morning. She asked me to call her the moment you awoke."

"Are you serious? What is her name? I ask pushing aside my breakfast things and giving her my full attention.

"She didn't say, but she has a Spanish accent. Perhaps she comes from Spain—no, maybe Mexico, or Brazil, something like that."

She pulls my cup back towards me, and with hand on hip, pours me more heavenly coffee. This lovely, multi-tasking French Madame truly is the right woman for her job. She has charm flowing from every orifice. I am hypnotized by her confidence, her ease and independence. Despite my travel clothes and graying hair, her elegance spills over and makes me feel beautiful again.

"So, *mon petite*, may I?" She emphasizes her question by raising one eyebrow and turning her shoulder towards me like some fifties icon posed with a coffee pot.

"Huh, what… Sorry, but what do you mean?" I mumble, totally embarrassed to be caught fawning.

Madame French Knickers is a professional muse, and pretends she doesn't notice. She is probably used to it. Again she repeats her question, "May I call her back, telling her that you are awake and able to take her call?"

"Oh yeah, sure, go ahead" I reply.

I am completely bewildered. I sip my coffee and eat from the plate of gorgeous food, all the while searching my mind over and over for who this could be. No one knows that I am here, only my parents. I made very sure of this before I left, for precisely one reason: I do not want company. This is my solo journey, my own private adventure and the last thing I want is unexpected fellow travelers. I start to think of the many ways I could avoid meeting this woman.

But then I hear, "Oui Madame, she is right here," and I am handed the telephone.

I tremble as I take the receiver, not sure if I am angry, frightened or excited. "Bonjour?"

The Latin voice on the end of the telephone begins to speak. "Sophia, I know who you are, and I am here to help you. You have to trust me. Come to Puivert. There are others here who are waiting for you. If you promise me that you will come, I will send you the key to my house."

"Are you sure you are speaking to the right person? Who are you? Have we met?" I ask suspiciously.

"No Sophia, we have not met. But I do know you. My name is Pythia. I know you have many questions, and I will give you many answers. But for now I do not have much time for talking. Sophia, you can trust me. Please come – I will send you the key."

Silence seems to fill the room, thick, warm and pulsing. The clatter of dishes and conversation is dulled. I hear Pythia breathing, I can feel Madame staring, and I can taste my own adrenalin, metallic on my tongue. Time ticks on. My mind is racing but my intuition is saying YES. Okay then.

"Yes Pythia, send me the key. I will come". I hear the click of the line going dead just before I hand the receiver back to Madame.

"Very good choice my darling. You have done the right thing."

She winks at me with dazzling composure. "Now go back upstairs and prepare yourself because I have a feeling that key will turn up sooner than you think."

In a complete daze, I turn and walk up the stairs with a very strange expression upon my face—sheer disbelief, mixed with amazement that things like this really do happen. In my room, I flop on the bed, dizzied by heavy waves of sleep. Whether I'm feeling jet lag, nervous tension, or altered consciousness I don't know, nor do I care. But I do know one thing. Everything is about to change!

The key fits the lock. With a deep, resonant click I turn the latch, pushing open the heavy, ornate wooden door as I cross the threshold of Maison Rouge, a neo-classical mansion nestled upon a hillside, high above the village of Puivert.

A Roman mosaic floor gleams up at me as I step into the entrance hall of the enigmatic home of Pythia. A vase of succulent red, pink and orange roses catches my attention, and the delicate waft of their perfume fills my nostrils. This place is huge: five stories high and there is probably a cellar beneath my feet. It feels cold, as if no one had lived here for a long time, and yet the roses are fresh and the floor sparkling clean. Suddenly a chill sweeps through me. Am I alone in this house? I recall my last conversation with Pythia, the one in the cab when she told me she would be in the States for three months, and that it would just be the me and the cats until she returned.

All is quiet, yet I do not feel alone. I feel as if a hundred eyes are upon me, watching and observing to see how I respond to this new reality. The presence doesn't feel malevolent or threatening. If anything, it feels familiar, as if I had been acquainted with the house a long, long time ago. My eyes widen as I breathe in that possibility. An unmoving silence verifies it. As I close the front door, the rich, deep sound of a lock turning behind me confirms that I have entered a realm of otherworldly dimensions. With a tingle of excitement, I commit to my full participation in the next stage of this unfolding journey.

I step across the mosaic tiles, which draw me like an intriguing puzzle. With mounting curiosity I push open the 1920's stained glass door that leads from the foyer into the mansion's mirrored salon. I smile to myself. Every nuance of Pythia's home is a reflection of how I imagine her to be: mysterious, timeless, regal and royal. It is no surprise to discover that her private residence is hidden away within the foothills of the Pyrenees Mountains, shrouded by the legendary stronghold of Montsegur and the enigmatic village of Rennes le Chateau. These walls feel like they hold dominion between the worlds. Here, the usual rules and regulations do not exist. I am abruptly realizing that Maison Rouge is a sovereign state just like its owner—free from the influence of Samael and his relentless psychic stalking.

Here I am safe. It dawns on me that Pythia has offered me refuge, shelter from the storm and comfort from the rain. My heart melts and once more I feel hungry, as if it is safe to eat again.

Most of the shutters are closed, permitting only the occasional shaft of sunlight to penetrate the darkness. While my eyes adjust I slowly gaze around the room, soaking up its elaborate atmosphere. Rich, warm tones of claret and gold emerge, reminding me of the

Baroque period exemplified by the palace of Versailles. Velvet brocade sofas and chaise lounges fill the room with grandeur. Exquisite pieces of Italian fine art hang from the walls in antique gold frames. I inhale deeply. Sumptuous, exotic aromas linger in the air, evoking forgotten memories of offerings and sacrifices made before an altar. Amazingly, this is all so familiar to me. Waves of nostalgia suddenly wash through me, arousing my carefully barricaded emotions. A huge sob escapes my lips and I reach for the worn leather armchair to steady myself.

Pythia, thank you! Thank you for bringing me to this place.

My thoughts drift back to that inexplicable moment when Pythia called me from out of nowhere. I still do not understand what this is all about but I do know that I am part of something greater. Something is orchestrating all of this, and trying to figure it out is a waste of time. There are some things in this world that cannot be comprehended by the mind, and this is definitely one of them. I smile as the grateful tears on my cheek seep into the corners of my mouth when I remember the sound of her voice. It was the clear, soft cadence of her Hispanic accent that drew my unflinching attention. She spoke with such tenderness that she instantly awakened my intuitive YES.

Sophia, I know who you are, and I am here to help you. You have to trust me. Come to Puivert. There are others here who are waiting for you. If you promise me that you will come, I will send you the key to my house. Let this burden lay upon my shoulders until you are strong enough to pick it up again...

Again I feel the intensity of that moment. I just *knew* that I could trust her.

The weight of something heavy resting in my hand pulls me

back into the present moment. I notice that I am still holding the wrought iron key of the front door, the very key that she had promised me. A wave of tiredness sweeps through me. My legs can't hold me up, and I sink into the welcoming embrace of a patiently waiting chair. I close my eyes and drop my bags to the floor. Even though my mind wants so desperately to rationalize the situation, it is my soul that speaks first. *You are one who has taken a path beyond the ordinary. Everything is waiting for you. Put down the weight of your aloneness, and see the good in yourself at last.* This resonant truth makes tears flow, and two black sludgy streaks of mascara course down my face, giving me the semblance of some ancient tribal warrior. Years of tension succumb to release and authenticity begins to stir inside me. The tears turn into a sob that threatens to never end. Here it comes at last. The tsunami of grief I have been running from.

I sit there heaving up my heavy load, while my ancestors gather round me looking on in wonder at what they were unable to do. Powerful oceanic waves of muck rise up into my heart as I cough and splurge it all out. My fingers claw at the sofa arms as the mother of all nauseas groans in my stomach. My eyes stretch as I gag at the enormity of this new emotion. Fear hisses at my back suggesting that I stop all this crying and look around the house for the kitchen. Ah ha I have caught you—the distraction technique! *Go to the kitchen, gorge on food and swallow back down your own shackles. Then quietly and shamefully vomit it out* ... No, not this time my compadre; this time I turn to my new alliance. Right now I am going to sink back down into this worn out armchair and give it all that I've got!

"Rooaaaarrrr!!!!" Cough, heave, spit ... Venomous words,

filthy language and vile sounds spew from my mouth, powerfully reverberating throughout all five floors of Maison Rouge. I remain sitting there, panting like a mother who has just given birth after twenty-two hours of labor. Sweat beads at my forehead, revealing a smile drenched in happiness that not only fills my face, but my soul. In the aftermath, I realize that all that I have never spoken has just left my lips. The dark veil begins to lift and slowly, slowly, slowly, fragments of light begin to glimmer all around me.

Thud!

My eyes are suddenly wide open. Something is moving inside the house. I stand up, wrapping my shawl around me for comfort and protection as I wipe my face. I quietly cross the lavish blood-red Moroccan rugs, go past the wood burning stove, and creep towards the cerise and plum canopied silk curtains covering two glass doors that seem to open up into the kitchen. *Thud!* Then I hear the clatter of pots and pans rolling across the floor. I stand still, almost frozen to the spot, as I prepare myself for whatever is about to happen next. Silence fills my ears. I strain to listen. Who or *what* is in the kitchen?

Moments later I am on the move again, drawing closer to the source of the unknown noise. Approaching the glass doors, I pull the curtain aside and peer through. I see no one, only a farmhouse style kitchen, complete with a maple island dressed with a vase of roses. Something else catches my eye. Next to the freestanding sink is a tray with a scroll tied with a red ribbon. Intuition tells me that this is a message left for me by Pythia. And yet, how curious, because she was already in the States when she called me. Realization dawns with a prickle of surprise. *She must have known that I was coming even before she asked …*

A cool breeze wafts against my left side, distracting me from my thoughts. I turn to see where it is coming from, and as my eyes adjust to the dim light, the centerpiece of the house reveals itself. Standing proudly before me is a grand oak staircase, complete with balustrades, leading elegantly to the upper floors. I catch my breath as the sheer enormity of the mansion engulfs me. Anything could be hiding here. The place is absolutely huge. I feel so small and exposed within these walls.

And what is in the kitchen? Finally, heart beating loudly, I push open one of the glass-paneled doors. Floor to ceiling windows reveal a medieval walled garden outside, and a crystal chandelier, which throws cascades of sunlight in every direction. I blink in the brightness, and there in the corner I see the culprit, her eyes wide and her tail long. Relieved beyond measure, and beaming from ear to ear, I crouch down to her level, holding out my hand to introduce myself. Delighted to see and feel such beauty before me, I find myself gazing into the hypnotic turquoise eyes of one of Pythia's Siamese cats. All the scary feelings of being in an unknown house leave, the moment I begin to stroke her back. The sound of her ecstatic purring fills the kitchen, and suddenly everything is right again in my world.

Time disappears into nonexistence as the day leisurely unfolds. All cares and concerns evaporate as I throw open all the shutters and usher new life into the house. By late afternoon, I have met all thirteen of Pythia's cats, and have aired all twenty-two of her rooms. To commemorate my first day at Maison Rouge, I open a bottle of the local Blanquette, squealing with delight as the cork explodes on the terrace. Savoring every sip, I luxuriate in the sheer self-indulgence of this elegant, amazing chateau. Leaning back in my bamboo lounger, I lift my glass to the plush lavender streaks that fill the deep red sky. *Here's to the next chapter!* With the utterance of these words, I begin to feel at *home.* Within minutes, I surrender into sweet sleep.

Come my love, let me bathe you.

His voice emerges from behind my right shoulder, creating waves of ecstasy that course through my body. *Take my hand and let me ease you into this bath, allow the sweetness of my love to melt you.* His voice holds the promise of healing. In the center of my being, I know that his touch will caress every wound until I am once again immaculate. Yet I am unable to open fully. The dark shadow of my past stands between us, obscuring the light of this grace. I am afraid. I doubt that this can be real. How can I believe again? Though somehow ... I do.

I turn around, expecting once again to be alone, but instead I see the shimmering form of a translucent man. My eyes languidly take in his presence. I watch him breathe, sending ripples of energy throughout the soft caresses of light that form his silhouette. *This is not a dream. This is real.* I continue to gaze, glued to the spot by the sheer power of his presence as swathes of pearlescent light radiate all around him. I am afraid I will lose consciousness within this dream, and cause it to prematurely end. I hasten to speak. *Who are you?*

I am the one who was sent to find you.

Something ancient whispers inside of me, *Ani L'Dodi.* I hear the words but do not recognize them. I look away, turning my head from his glorious appearance, as feelings of shame shackle my aching body. I cannot discern his face or his features, as they are irradiated by light—and yet I can see them. He is paradoxically visible and invisible. It would be right to say he is *known.* This *knowingness* causes a montage of sensation within me, as I wrestle with feelings of unworthiness and reunion.

With exceptional effort, I turn back to him and open the cold, heavy doors of my resistance. I take his hands and nod in acceptance. The moment our hands touch, warm rushes of tingling energy rush up the length of my arms, penetrating the over-protective walls of my heart, awakening the fragile memories of our original separation. I gasp as slithers of his love enter my soul. Finally I step into the warm fragrant waters that await me. Plumes of Jasmine and Frankincense rise up in vapours that swirl and drag me deeper into the bathtub, causing torrents of bath water to pour over the edge. Releasing his hands, I descend into darkness, sinking deeper into this womb-like world, praying for the tumultuous eons of my journey to evaporate.

What is your name?

Deeper and deeper I sink into the black velvet liquid light. In some far, far away place I hear his voice. *Logos.*

Logos. *Logos* … My mind is now switched off. I begin to freely wander through the sensational world of palpable communion. I don't need to breathe anymore—in this place life, death, good and bad roll into one voluptuous reality. I am in a vast, living midnight sky that is starless and black, with a delicate sensation of the universe gently pressing upon me. An arc of flame gracefully emerges from out of the velvety darkness. A fire of gold, liquid in flow, space in substance, unfolds and pulls me in. A sea of glass rolls open, an unfurling magic carpet in an ocean of light. Flecks of liquid fire course through this ocean of brilliance. Angels with wings on their faces and thousands of eyes peer at me, convulsing me in orgasmic shivers.

Wonderstruck, I bow in reverence to the majesty of it all.

His hands reach into the water, gently lifting me back to the surface. I am unable to speak, unable to think, I am unborn and yet can see that he is holding an old Victorian pewter jug in one hand and tenderly caressing an iridescent solution with the other.

This water comes from our true home, the place where we come from. May I pour it over you?

In that moment a cascade of stars soars through my heart. *Our true home. Oh my, oh my—, oh my Beloved God ... I remember, my sweet love, I remember!* Symbols of remembrance flash through my soul: The rapture of peacocks and the howl of rabid dogs churn within me. I don't want to avoid this any longer—let me feast my eyes on the full glory and the full horror of the tumultuous reality that I am one with. I am all things! I know this without thinking; I understand all ... I am sumptuous, tender, drenched with beauty, radiant and wildly fecund. At the same time I am terrifying— chaotic, horrible, devastating and harsh. I am ALL of it, radiating and spinning together in full force. The more I remember, the wider my eyes become.

Then, my Beloved pours the cascade of homecoming over my heart and breasts, causing my skin to tingle and bead. Every fibre of my being revels in orgasmic bliss. Tenderness, mercy, redemption, forgiveness, glory and victory surge through my veins, cracking open the quantum nature of my entire existence. Space peels back and dissolves into blazing radiance. Coruscating cornucopias of colors dazzle my eyes, blinding and revealing all at once. I gasp in awe as the ocean of light coalesces into a gleaming diamante sphere that explodes and implodes within me simultaneously.

The rapt reverie ends. In exquisite slow motion he stands up and steps away from the bath. He gazes at me with a penetrating sobriety.

My darling Sophia. The truth is I came for you ...

But it was you who came for all ...

I can hear the white noise of silence. I feel its pressure. Then my physical body's instinctual urge to breathe catapults me into three-dimensional reality. I am back on the terrace, gasping and yearning. And somehow I know it is true.

I came for all.

Chapter 13

Return of the She King

His mount paws the ground, sending stardust in every direction. A loud guttural snort ruptures the silence, sending forth plumes of heated trepidation that ripple out across the universe. *Something is moving down there, something is stirring on Earth.* An unspoken knowing quivers between creature and rider. *The quickening is coming!*

His black-leathered fingers squeeze the reins, steadying them both for what could come next. Cloaked in a black hood, the Logos sits like a nobleman keeping watch over the land, holding vigil over the realm. He cannot be seen in the darkness of deep space. Only the occasional ripple of energy hints at His presence. He had agreed to conceal His light in order to maintain the delicate balance of Creation. Universal chaos could result if his great Light were fully revealed, for paradoxically His presence wields the power to destroy all mortals. Direct, blinding contact with His unmasked Love Light could cause such excruciating pain that they would perish on the spot. Thus it is best for all life that the Logos hides in the shadows whilst the lower dimensions move around him, totally unaware of just how close their Beloved Divine One actually is.

There is only one who can bear him, and that is His beloved Sophia. Memories of Her flood his awareness. A faint smiled forms upon his lips as he remembers the way He would watch Her move, how His light would catch Her face and drop Him to His knees. It was She who brought such tremendous joy and love to the Pleroma. Everywhere She moves, She brings ecstasy, for She is Love—the total embodiment of that great Holy Force. She is the Divine Mother, the one who warms the heart with raptures of grace, mercy and belonging. Without her, there is no joy, no life. Nothing is the same.

His heart weighs heavy in His chest. His throat tightens and burns with unaccustomed tears. This newfound emotion drives His quest. Closing his eyes, He searches the darkness to find Her.

My Beloved, where are you? Please show me a sign so I may find you. Please grant me the knowledge of how to take this first step.

A faint waft of stardust caresses His face. In answer to His heartfelt prayer, an inner dimension opens up before Him. He sees Sophia sleeping in a large bed covered in cats. They are on the bed beside Her and also forming a circle on the floor. *They are guarding Her.* In His vision, he stands in the room as She sleeps. The cats see him, but do not move. He walks to the window and glances outside at the awaiting mountains. Tall and majestic, they are green and blossoming. A sound catches His ear. She is mumbling in Her sleep. He swiftly moves to the bedside and reaches for Her hand, but He is unable to take it. He is in one world, and She is in the other. Standing beside the bed, He gazes down at Her face with joy, yet hot stabs of separation remind Him that His odyssey is far from over.

As He stands frozen in yearning, He begins to speak. These

words rise up from an ancient place within Him—a place He thought had died long ago.

His resonant voice fills the room. "As I gaze upon you, I see all the Edens that have fallen in me, all the Paradises that were once in my hands, and all the Heavens I had to let go.

"I see the promises that I did not keep, the pains I did not soothe, the wounds I did not heal and the tears I did not shed. I see the deaths of those I did not mourn, the prayers I did not answer, the doors I did not open, and the doors I did not close.

I see all that was offered to me, and all the things that I could not accept. I see all that could have been, and all that never will be."

Deep, deep in regret the Logos is now on bended knee openly weeping, openly sobbing in ways that only a human ever could.

Slowly, Sophia opens her eyes. Her hand reaches toward His, yet it is a phantom hand one that He cannot grasp.

"Logos—are you there?"

The sound of Sophia's weakened voice cruelly shatters Him. The sight of Her lost eyes haunts Him, touching places inside that make Him cringe. *Her light! Her light is so … dim, so bleak and fragile.* She is not as He remembers. Pierced with compassion, He calls from His heart, *Oh my love, I pray that I reach you in time!*

This huge burst of feeling and despair catapults Him forcefully out of the vision. He is back in the black void between worlds, waiting on His mount with full recognition of the enormous task before them. But this was no horse that He sat upon, for this creature has been trained to endure Him and His quest. The Logos and his Dragon are two hearts sealed in perfect union. Forged in the fires of the Pleroma, His Dragon feels what He feels, and what

His Dragon senses, He does as well. Together they are bound as one to find Her. Now, their time of inaction is almost over. For too long they have endured the cold emptiness of deep space. For too long they have stood still waiting—waiting for Her to awaken.

The Dragon's tail undulates, gathering energy for a swift and mighty descent. The Logos throws His head back, communing with His Dragon through imagery and sensation. Powerful reverberations of energy flood into the Logos. Gasping for breath He and the Dragon simultaneously see Her, and feel what She felt just before she — . *Descended.*

The Logos unsheathes His sword and projects the blade up, holding the hilt with both hands as He roars out into the darkness, "I *shall* find Her, and when I do, I shall bring Her home!" The light of His words explodes into the void, but is almost immediately extinguished. How strange. The Logos and his Dragon draw closer into union, as the scarlet gold eyes of the dragon glint wildly and his tail thrashes madly.

The darkness is getting stronger. The balance is tipping; their Light is being overshadowed. This can mean only one thing.

The *Descent* had begun.

Beneath the folds of His hood He closes His eyes and prays. The Logos and His Dragon are an unyielding force, but the idea of descending troubles them – greatly. Their hearts pound in unison. Adrenalin pulses through their veins. Gravity pulls at their souls. Heaviness floods their bodies and attempts to squeeze the Light from them. As His irradiating presence begins to diminish, the Logos pulls back his hood and tears off His cloak to reveal the full majesty of His Light. A blaze of splendor fills the darkness. His Dragon rains molten fire into the yawning abyss that swiftly opens before them. In the blink of an eye they disappear!

Together the Logos and his Dragon slip into the black light of the deep embracing abyss. At first the descent feels effervescent, bubbling through Him, consuming Him, until all sense of Himself dissolves. He descends to the bottom, lying motionless, like a fading star just inches from the ground. Floating there in the veiled darkness, obscured like a submerged precious stone, He notices that He is alone. With that realization He lands heavily on the ground.

The shock overwhelms him. For the first time, he cries *real* tears of pain. He had been forewarned that he would become human, but this taste of the mortal wound of separation is unspeakably bitter. His tears are those of a *man* discovering aloneness for the first time. The full-blown reality of this moment hits him face on, and his pain is amplified. Suddenly the face of Sophia appears against a backdrop of demons, withered and wretched. She cries out to him, and her voice tears his heart open. He falls to the ground in prostration and helpless despair. The dire reality of their separation now registers fully in both the human and Divine aspects of himself. It rips him apart, and he only has one option.

He prays, really prays, for his transforming Light to arrive. His prayer begins as a whisper, then turns into a voice, and finishes as a blood-curdling scream!

"I beseech Thee O Nameless One, please, please help me!"

As the Logos cries out for his salvation, the redeeming force in his blood begins to bubble and transform. He feels himself becoming lighter and softer. He is thrown backwards as shafts of transformational light penetrate His brain, reactivating his divinity and grace. A crescendo of intensity fills his newly physical body. He stretches and arches to accommodate the heavenly frequency.

He jerks and shudders as the Divine Light reaches out across the planet to encompass Him.

He undulates and reels with ecstasy as He bequeaths his loving gratitude to His Father. "Oh thank God, oh thank God!"

Over and over, praise pours from His lips as beads of sweat roll down His cheeks. Then He is silenced. Humbled, He tries to some make sense of it all. But none comes, only the horrific realization that the human soul is so far away from home. He sighs in utter weariness, knowing that His journey has only just begun.

The Logos slowly stands up. His eyes roll towards the sky in sheer disbelief. *I am here. I have made it.* He exhales, releasing particles of alchemical manifestation, as He majestically breathes *air* into His lungs for the first time. He looks down at His outstretched hands, turning them over as he examines His new form. He is not quite human. He is more like a *ghost.* Made of light and translucent flesh, as if made of liquid rather than skin and bone. He touches His head, tracing the shape and contours of His face, feeling the eye sockets and nose and the watery opening of His mouth. He is some strange mix of human and Divine. He is not entirely sure whether this was what the Nameless One envisioned.

To the beholder on Earth, He is a true and rare beauty. Strong, well formed and filled with a profound elixir that transforms all that is corrupt and cruel into a haven of light. His hair is fair and slightly curled, falling just past his shoulders, while his cobalt blue eyes light up like precious jewels that bring all bitterness to an end. Light irradiates Him from within, casting a hue of Paradise that brings comfort to all who bathe in it. He is beautiful and He is unyielding.

Deep within His inner ear He senses the rapid approach of

something familiar, yet strange. He grabs the hilt of His sword and turns. A tremendous light explodes before Him, almost blinding His delicate eyes. Shielding His face from the blast of white heat He staggers backward and raises His sword. A trillion particles of screaming sound trumpet before Him. Then a surge of fiery heat embraces Him.

"Grraaaaagh!" The thunderous rasp of His own Dragon fills his ears. And at once they race towards one another in rapturous reunion. Eventually the Logos pulls back and inspects the new appearance of His dragon. Slowly and deliberately He walks all around him, muttering to himself and rubbing his jaw. The dragon's body is completely covered with tough, shiny scales that include every imaginable shade of emerald green and burnished gold. He is wearing a gold breastplate encrusted in jewels to protect His soft underbelly and chest. The scales are pentagonal teardrops. The logos laughs out loud when He sees how His dragon can make them stand on end whenever He wishes. He rubs His dragon's shoulder as an act of respect and admiration, and in response the dragon extends His wings to full reach and shoots wild fire into the darkening sky.

The Logos stands before His dragon, looking Him directly in the eye. He prefers to communicate through the senses rather than spoken words. Thus He shares His concerns. *He has seen Sophia, and He is sure that She has seen Him too.* He shows the Dragon how very dim Her light is, and how fragile and unprotected She seems. Together they stand motionless, listening to the inner and the outer worlds whilst communing as one, enabling shared insights.

The dragon sniffs at the air, extracting their precise location threaded within nature's wisdom. *He and the Logos are in the Northern Hemisphere, on the continent called Europe.* He sniffs again, searching for time coordinates and seasonal positioning. Again nature responds sending forth knowledge into the instinctual center located deep within the dragon's belly. *It is 2014 and it is late Spring.*

A third inhale to locate the scent of Sophia, or any creature that has seen Her. *Which direction do we go?* the dragon silently asks.

West, towards the French Pyrenees, comes the reply. Yet this voice is not sourced in the Dragon's intuitive belly. It is strange, but somewhat familiar. A human. A woman—Pythia.

The scarlet eyes of the Dragon widen in surprise, as the golden yellow slit narrows and almost disappears. He can now hear a human praying. It is a man, but something is not right. This prayer is directly affecting his Master! He rasps and screams, stamping His clawed feet in defiance, unsure what is happening but hell-bent on protecting his own.

"It is okay dear one, all is happening as it should be. Do not fear your Master's journey, for you shall be together. Relax and let go!" The woman's voice strangely soothes him.

The voice of the man's prayer grows stronger. "Dear Lord, please fill me with your light and courage! Please help me face what I need to face!" The man's call grows in intensity, filling the space between them, and as the Dragon watches helplessly, the Light of the Logos grows weaker. His ghostly form dims, and in a heartbeat He is gone!

The Logos has been pulled by the power of the man's prayer, and unwittingly jumps into the man's human body, only minutes away from where Sophia is sleeping! From far, far away, the Nameless One chuckles at the perfection of this Earthly drama. The Dragon feels a tremendous force pulling Him again towards His Master. In a split second He is transformed into a Czechoslovakian wolf dog. Smaller in stature, yet filled with an indomitable spirit he finds himself pressing his furry bulk against the thigh of the now, *very human* Logos.

In a darkened temple, deep in the primordial belly of the earth, Pythia sits with her black obsidian ball, carefully watching the events unfold. All around her are mystical symbols and indecipherable calculations. Her life has lead her to this moment, a moment she was born to live. She has been in a trance for days, tended to by three of her handmaidens. Soaked in sweat and shaking profusely she returns to the land of the living with a smile that revivifies her maiden's faith.

"It is done," she whispers.

Chapter 14

Requiem of Illusion

My eyes open like a little girl's on Christmas morning, full of excitement and eager to live the day. Enjoying this warm moment of anticipation, I snuggle further down into the bed and peer out from over the top of the velvet brocade bed spread. A smile appears on my lips. I feel safe in this amazingly opulent bedroom.

It is enormous and filled with light, as the morning sun streams in through shimmering silk drapes. There are three sets of huge glass terrace doors leading out to a balcony. The floor looks like it is made from paneled walnut and it is partly covered in thick, exotic Persian and Moroccan rugs. Half of this massive bedroom has exposed timber and stone walls; the other half is upholstered in delicious velveteen rose fabric. There are artifacts and art pieces that span centuries and continents just in this one room! Shaking my head in wonderment, I continue investigating from the warmth of my bed. The sun may be shining, but the cool morning chill reminds me that the Pyrenees Mountains are near.

This moment is perfect. I can feel others on the bed with me and raise my head up a bit more to see *five* cats dotted in various positions on the velvet brocade. Little tears bead at the corner my eyes in a wave of gratitude for the comfort of this extraordinary hospitality. As I lie back down, the dream from last night suddenly appears in my head, again creating an insatiable desire within me. Life force surges through my veins, as I grab the sheets between my fingers. My eyes close and roll up inside my head as the image of him fills me once more. My heart feels like it is being prized open by a hungry god, desperate to feel human again. I arch backwards to create more space in my chest so I can breathe. Gasping and spluttering I allow these feelings to rise to the surface.

I am protected here, and finally there is no one around to listen except the cats. So I howl, I groan, I cry out—I surrender to the realization that I love this man, this *being*, more, more, more than anything I have ever known—and if I do not meet him I will surely die.

The more I surrender, the stronger he becomes. I know in absolute certainty that he is my true Beloved. He is a being who not only radiates Divine presence but augments that with his willingness to experience sacred relationship at the most edgy and incandescent levels. He is a man who is prepared to go to the depths of the Mystery and the wonder of Love. A man who can plumb the darkness of desire to find gold which is then refined from that dark boiling cauldron and offered to the service of the world. I sense him so strongly...

Is he already here? The thought sends me over the edge.

His presence seems to fill the bedroom and I burn with a craving I have never known before. I open my eyes and sit bolt upright in bed looking at the spot where he was ...*Who is he?* My mind frantically searches for the word, *beginning with L? Logos!* Yes. I look at the spot where Logos was kneeling.

"Logos—are you there?" I repeat my words from last night.

I know that this wasn't a dream—it was real. My brain races, trying to fathom what on earth could be going on. *Have I gone insane, am I depressed, am I delusional, is he a ghost?* Despite my mind's attempt to create some kind of order and control over the situation—there really is none. All I have is the powerful feeling of the experience—and that is enough to last a million lifetimes.

It has been so long since I have felt *any* kind of feeling! And now in just two days, the floodgates are down. It feels crazy, but good, and I have a vague, distant memory that this state of rapture is *normal* for me. Wheee! I am free to feel this ecstatic longing. I am free to let my mind wander and to let my passions loose. I can feel my brain cells firing up and my biochemistry going haywire – and I don't care!

I open my arms and lean my head back, exposing my throat and heart as a demonstration of my surrender. I pray aloud for the whole world to hear.

"My Love, my Love, come, come, come to me. Find me, I beg of you! I shall know you by the Light in your eyes, as you are the one that awaits me at the end of my crucible."

Resounding silence engulfs my words, leaving me utterly spent with a ringing tone in my ears. Then I have a distinct memory jog. *Wait a second! I have heard those words before! I remember now… I called to Him when I was staying at Mom and Dad's. Yes, on the morning I filed for divorce! I had a daydream about a man—a knight or warrior with whom I'd made some kind of pact!*

A wave of happiness and wonder washes through me as I can

see how far I have already come. I marvel at the great Force orchestrating my life. It sure as hell surpasses anything I could ever have dreamed up! Gratitude fills my heart again as I recognize that I am indeed healing. *I am retrieving all parts of my original self and becoming who I really am!* I rest in the tingling throws of delicious, genuine happiness.

Many, many deep breaths later, I begin the excitement of exploring the rest of this amazing house. I notice an imposing wardrobe standing next to the marble fireplace opposite the balcony doors. What an ornate and antique masterpiece of fine art masquerading as piece of furniture! Painted in peppermint and lavender, this richly sculpted clothes cupboard simply begs to be opened. I pull a glittery silver blanket over my shoulders and rise from bed. The cats jump and purr around me. The doors open with a whoosh of tantalizing scent. *Pythia!* I can feel her presence emanating from the beautiful clothing inside. I send her a heartfelt *thank you* and continue exploring.

The tall windows call me, and I pull back a drape to take a quick peek outside. I am greeted with the breathtaking scene of the walled garden, a glorious lake and the majestic view of the Château de Puivert in the distance. I imagine seeing myself from the garden down below—the classic image of a solitary woman using a curtain to hide her modesty. I see how insignificantly small I am at the window of this incredibly large mansion. *How will Logos ever find me?* I smile at myself, bemused and drinking in the beauty before me, totally lost in questions that are beyond any hope of an answer.

Ring ring!

Oh my God! The strident call of my cell phone completely startles me. I'm not expecting any calls! The sound is almost alien to my ears. I scramble for my purse and fumble inside, pulling everything out all over the bed. *Got it.*

"Hello?" I enquire.

"It's Pythia. I have something very grave to tell you. I have just been informed that Samael is in France and he is looking for you. He knows that we are in contact with each other and he is very threatened by this."

My breath contracts. "Whaaaa—"

"Don't ask me any questions, Sophia. Just listen and prepare yourself. He will arrive later today. I'm sorry. He knows my address. Now my dear, there is more. I had hoped that I would have more time to prepare you for this, but that luxury is not with us anymore. I must tell you now, before you see him. Sophia, listen closely. You are more than just an ordinary woman. You are Divine—the Holy Sophia herself. You have fallen from the Heavens to come to Earth to retrieve all aspects of yourself …"

Overwhelm, disbelief and a tingle of fear cause me to shut down. I begin to drift off, despite the urgency of Pythia's voice. I collapse on the bed, keep the cell phone at my ear, close my eyes and pass out, willing some deep part of myself to remember everything … By the time I come to, my head feels like it's going to explode. The cell phone has been pressed against my ear and it is hot from radio waves. Pythia told me so many things, but it's all a blur in my conscious mind. It's all a mad, wild, crazy, incoherent— but familiar—blur.

Before I know it, there is a hard and opposing knock at the door that casts a shadow across the house. My heart quickens. *I know who this is—I would know that intensity of intrusion anywhere!* The usual rush of fear encircles me, and old habits of intimidation attempt to render me paralyzed. Like a blackened, smoldering hell dog, the fear lingers in the shadows, yet it's afraid to step into the light.

I stand utterly still for a moment, trying to center and remember everything Pythia told me. I force myself to breathe deeply. I am a *Divine* being. I remember that—over and over, she emphasized that I must step into my true power. With a strong prayer, I summon the strength I am going to need in the coming moments. I summon my Self! Everything comes flooding back, faster than I can comprehend. I see clearly now that the next chess piece has moved into position. It's time to face the music, pull off the mask and quit bullshitting around with some kind of victim story.

He knocks again, this time much harder and even more insistent! I can feel him seething, itching to rage at me, desperate to reinforce his belief that he is powerful and that there is no one above him.

But that isn't going to happen today. Today the veils come down. Today the truth of *why* we had a relationship, and the reason for that insanely obsessive *attraction* shall be revealed. I can't believe I am doing this. I can't believe I am going to open the door and let him in. But I know I must. In a sudden epiphany, I realize that our disastrous marriage and hellish divorce is actually symbolic of something far greater, something that has far reaching consequences. Though I don't fully understand yet, I am left knowing one thing—what happens next is going to be epic.

My heart pounds as I get close to the door. Memories of my past fill my head. I know how fearsome he can be. I want to turn away and not answer the insistent knock. But it's too late—that option doesn't exist anymore. I breathe and square my shoulders in the great hall. The person who opens that door will not be my fearful old self, but none other than the Holy Sophia, Herself. *Oh, God help me.* I reach out with both hands to turn the golden doorknob and pull open the gilded wooden door. There he is.

The hot and violent barrage begins. "So this is where you ran away to? Mmm not bad ... but not yours," Samael hisses as he takes in the enormity of the house. "I need to talk to you, Pussycat" Without waiting for my invitation he walks right in.

Still the same old Samael, I think to myself. But I am not the same old Sophia.

He looks darker than I remember, and his unforgettable eyes bore into me: dark, penetrating and unyielding. He is dressed head to toe in black (no surprises there) in a military-style black wool frock coat with tails and silver buttons fastened all the way up. He had always been very well dressed, which pleased him greatly. I remember whenever we were at a social engagement he would constantly pluck his cuffs and collar for imaginary specs of dust. When he wasn't preening he would be smoothing his goatee over and over with his thumb and first finger like some kind of blue-blooded aristocrat. Yet now, despite his impeccable appearance, dark circles under his eyes suggest that he is smoking again. I watch him walk into the kitchen and disappear.

"So, Samael what brings you Southern France?" I say casually, as I stride after him. I am pretending that it's the most natural thing in the world to have my soon-to-be-ex-husband sitting at the kitchen table, even though I left him months ago on the other side of the planet. "And how did you know I was here?" I ask lightly, throwing out bait to see where and when it will take the bite.

"I think you know the answer to both those questions" he replies while tapping his antique Japanese lighter on the kitchen table. *He is nervous, anxious to get down to it.*

"Well, yes, I probably do" I answer, as I switch the kettle on. "I guess it's the same way I found out that you were coming. You want coffee?" I ask.

He ignores my question. "So, you knew I was coming, eh? Well, let me take a teeny guess who you've been talking to. I would say it was your *little buddy* Pythia who has been telling tales about us."

He emphasizes the words *little buddy* to purposely show his disrespect for her, knowing damn well that she is a high level prophetess and oracle. He always does this; he puts people down to criticize and humiliate them so he can feel bigger, greater and more important. This also instills doubt—his favorite trump card.

I can see clearly that he is trying to get me to think that Pythia had spoken to both of us. However, I know it isn't true. She had even warned me that he would say this, although I didn't need warning. I already know how he works. I've had time to unravel it.

Unfortunately, when we first met, he applied this particular method to all of my friends, and I fell for it. He has taught me well about the power of doubt. I know the way it leads to distrust—one of the most powerful human fears. This is how he works: doubt, distrust and divide. The 3D death machine. My heart lurches in unexpected compassion as I realize that this is all he knows. *Because this is how I made him.* We are both an intrinsic part of this design.

"Anyway Pythia is not important. But this is!" He pulls an envelope from inside his jacket pocket, and opens a formal looking letter. "This is a legal contract stating that you shall revoke all entitlements to my estate, finances and property. It also declares that you will not speak about any of this to any of the press or any persons in actual fact. Finally, you are to pay back everything I have given you."

He smirks at me. "I have worked out the amount. It comes to twenty thousand, five hundred twelve dollars and forty-six cents exactly. So—how would you like to pay?" I can see how much he is enjoying this. Then he shoves the papers towards me and adds, "Oh, and if you could just sign here."

I look at him in stunned silence. Unbelievable. Incredible. Now the truth can really be seen and *felt*. There is no shred of love between us. None whatsoever. I had thought, or rather *hoped* that perhaps there could remain a real piece of genuine affection as we went our separate ways. But now I see that is just part of the illusion I invented for myself.

I look Samael in the eye and say, "Do your best, try to destroy me. You see—I've already been to hell and back so many times that I must admit it's kind of boring." I sign the papers, and feel strangely free.

He starts to laugh. He sniggers at first and then lets out a full hearty bellow. "So Sophia, how far are you going to get now? I do believe you have nothing. Any money or savings left?"

He is pure vile.

I turn away and to hide my feelings. I am tasting a deep and dreadful sense of remorse with no sign of redemption. Aghast, I lean against the kitchen island for support as the truth sinks in a little deeper. I want to run away and leave him there, but I won't do it. I have already done that too many times. I feel a boiling, swirling rampaging storm brewing inside of me and I don't know where to turn. I feel like I'm going mad with all these stories.

I don't know what's real anymore. Who am I? Which story is true? Is it the one of an abusive marriage and divorce? Or is it the story of the Holy Sophia and her quest to retrieve human souls? My head swirls as sickness rises in my stomach. My mind is splitting and fragmenting into a million pieces. I cover my lips with the back of my hand in case I vomit. I feel like I am going to pass out.

I hear Samael huff. "Now what little game are you playing Sophia? What's wrong? Can't you face the truth that Pythia lied to you? Your nice little fantasy world isn't half as true as you would like it to be." His pure venom hits me, sending an excruciating cramp throughout my stomach.

Suddenly I hear Pythia's voice in my heart. *Sophia, it is only in Samael's presence that you will be able to integrate the truth of what I am telling you. It will feel terrible; it will be the worst kind of pain you can feel. You will feel as if you are going to be shattered into a million pieces. That is the time to hold steady and pray. For the truth is—you are here this time to make yourself whole. And this is the gift he brings you.* I groan in agony. Crazy. But I know deep inside the marrow of my bones that she is telling me the truth. This is my breaking point. Something has to change. And so I drop to my knees and pray.

In a thunderous voice that shatters my queasiness, I cry out, "O Light of Lights! I have had faith in you from the very beginning! Hear me now, O Light, as I pray for your help, for ignorance has entered me. I came to Earth to save our children, but instead I found myself surrounded by the darkness. I became unable to return. I have lost my Light and I have been tormented and vilified. Yet I have never stopped crying out for your help, though I fear my prayers did not reach you. Forgive me, O Light, for I have done things that I am ashamed to tell you."

The kitchen is silent, profoundly silent. I feel different. I feel calm, centered and ready. I stand up and brush the dust off my knees before I walk over to the terrace doors where Samael is standing. He has his back to me, but I can *feel* him sensing my every move.

"Samael, I have been told many things in the last days. I know who I am and how I can bring us both back to the Light." My voice is slow, soft and palpable. I stand there waiting for him to respond.

He turns to face me with dark cloudy eyes. He is desperately trying to maintain his composure. "You?" he screams. "*You* bring *us* back to the light? I *am* the Light! It is I who am God; there is none apart from me!"

I walk towards the front door calmly. I know he will follow. He hates it when I walk away from him. *Now I understand why.* It terrifies him to be ignored.

A powerful surge of energy pummels its way through me, filling my entire being with an astounding clarity and wisdom. My eyes open to a higher level of perception. I see Samael change into a lion-faced serpent. I see myself; I am becoming Sophia. I am the Mother of all Creation. I am the Sacred Feminine on Earth, Light made Matter, embodied Wisdom, Creatrix of the Realm, and Mother of Mercy. I thread my arm through Samael's and guide him to the front door. I open it, and send him outside.

"You are mistaken, Samael" I whisper before closing the door firmly behind him. I stand in the hall, my atoms spinning with Love and the power of ten billion Suns. I see clearly! This shining redemption has been delivered by the last person I ever expected.

Thank you Samael. What a paradox. As the darkness becomes light, the unsteady ground that once terrified me is now perfect, exhilarating and true.

Chapter 15

Deliverance

I am trying to come to terms with what is happening. I feel like I have suddenly been launched into some half-finished movie as the leading lady. At the same time, I am not entirely surprised with my stellar role. For if I go deep enough, I must admit that I have always known something like this would happen, even though it's so completely far out! Yet— here's the catch—it is so totally normal as well.

Ever since I escorted Samael to the door, I have been rattling around this great big house, trying to find a place where I can be comfortable enough to rest and let it all fall into place. Yet every time I sit down, I stand up again. I am swinging like a pendulum. One moment I'm beginning to consciously accept and integrate what Pythia told me; then in the next moment I deny it all. I am totally alone in this difficult internal battle. There is absolutely no one to talk to except the cats! Even if there was someone around, the question is—would I tell the whole bizarre story? I don't even think that I could. I mean, come on—where do you start?

Now my dear, there is more. I had hoped that I would have

more time to prepare you for this, but that luxury is not with us anymore. I must tell you now, before you see him. Sophia, listen closely. You are more than just an ordinary woman. You are Divine —the Holy Sophia herself. You have fallen from the Heavens to come to Earth to retrieve all aspects of yourself ... Pythia's words haunt me and beg me to remember all that she said. Exhausted from trying to work it out in my mind, I take my journal, pen and blanket, and finally collapse into an awaiting armchair.

Closing my eyes, I do my best to scribble down everything I remember. My hand moves quickly across the page. *Pythia said that I am the Holy Spirit, and how the original meaning of my name Sophia means 'wisdom'—and that this* wisdom *is the Nameless One's consort. I, Sophia, am the feminine aspect of God and the Queen of the Heavenly realms!* Oh God. I stop writing and close my eyes. It is waaay too much to comprehend. My brain feels like it is going to explode ... and yet my heart feels strangely at home. *How on earth could the Holy Sophia be inside this petite human form,* I think in bemused denial as I look down at my curled up body. Then a wave of anger surges up.

"No! I can't do it!" I shout in frustration as I tear my sheet of paper away from the journal and screw it up into a ball. I throw it as far away from me as possible. But it bounces on the shiny floor and doesn't go away. How can I just toss this aside? I can't. Somehow I just have to face it, ludicrous as it sounds. Somehow, I must go forward with as much strength and dignity as I can find.

A shadow fills my mind. It is heavy and old, and carries with it the burden of responsibility, as well as the burden of success. The onus is on me whichever way I turn, it is here waiting for me. I soberly realize that from this moment onwards I carry the weight of the world upon my shoulders, and that no one will ever understand what that feels like. I feel achingly separate from life. None of my human rites of passage hold as much value now: the high and lows of material wealth, having a family, buying a house, creating a painting, even dying! All this is snatched away and suddenly replaced with an insurmountable task. I feel stripped of my human experience! I feel short-changed when I think of all the great ideas and plans that I had made for my simple little life. I sink into the armchair and groan, as the bliss of ignorance slides away through my fingers.

After some time, I return to my journal and try again to scribble down the essence of what Pythia had said. *Sophia was the first thought of the Nameless One. She was the first thing that He brought into existence. But after some time, Sophia—wisdom— had a curiosity to create something on Her own without the Nameless One's permission. What She did not realize was that Her every thought would become born, and so that curious thought became a 'child'—created in secret, without the Light of God. She was immediately ashamed and afraid of what happened. Her first reaction was to abort him. She attempted to cover up Her actions by turning away and wishing it had never happened. Because Her child did not contain God's light, AND because She rejected him, Her son became an aborted monster. He despised Her for what She had done and turned against Her.*

He decided to take his anger out on Her other creations, the human beings that She had created with the Nameless One. This angry, incomplete son came to Earth with a plan to corrupt and damage Her children. His plan was devious, though, because he also wanted to tempt Her to intervene. His plan worked. She came to Earth and found him waiting for Her. When in the Pleroma, She had no idea what had become of him on Earth, and She was not prepared for how powerful he had become.

Deep inside, Sophia was still ashamed, so She refused to call for help. She imagined and hoped that She could clear up her own mess and put things into their right place. Her idea was to fragment into a million, trillion pieces and place a piece of her Self inside each and every single human soul. It was a beautiful plan, but the moment She fragmented, She opened herself up for the worst possible outcome. Her son, now known as the Demiurge (controller of the material world), had created seven of his own 'children,' known as archons. These archons were not human; they were loveless beings, known in the Bible as seven deadly sins. Together, they schemed up ways to steal Her power and diminish Her Light, causing Her to fall further into the hell realms. The more the Demiurge stole Her light and rendered Her blind to Her Self, the weaker She grew. She became so lost in density that She completely forgot who She was and where She came from. Then, just when it looked like She would lose all of Her Light and fall completely into the abyss of darkness, She cried out to the Nameless One in prayers of repentance, confessing all that She had done, and asking for help.

The Nameless One responded immediately by sending forth The Logos, Her redeeming Light. Some say that when Jesus died and was placed in his tomb he went to the hell realms where Sophia was trapped, and rescued Her before he resurrected. That is why Christ said He must go away for the comforter to come to us. He had to descend to the darkest pit and rescue the Holy Spirit so she could be released into the hearts of those in the world.

My last paragraph is a misshapen scrawl that only I can

decipher. I pull the blanket closer and snuggle into the comforting armchair that seems to embrace me. Tired, lonely, frustrated tears streak down my face. I fall asleep, actually hoping I will never awake. Through veils and mists in my Dreamtime, I find myself in a beautiful woodland. I feel lighter and happier. I wander around enjoying the simplicity, the freedom and the ease of being that fills my body.

Up ahead of me, I see a dark Hispanic woman walking towards me with her arms outstretched in a welcoming gesture. *It is Pythia!* Her skin is olive and her hair long. She is wearing a dark hooded cloak that billows open as she walks. Underneath her cloak she is wearing an ornate saffron caftan, with a deep V-neck held in place by delicate gold ties. Her dark hair forms two cascades of tumbling curls that frame her voluptuous form. The closer she comes the more I can see her eyes—luminous golden pools that radiate loving wisdom. I am utterly comforted by her presence. All anguish and bitterness dissolve, leaving behind pure innocence and eagerness to serve.

She *knows* me, she *knows* what I am living, and she has *faith* that I can do this. A burning desire to rush towards her engulfs me, for she is my refuge, my sanctuary and my solace. She reaches for my hand and leads me over towards some rocks where we sit together for a long time just looking into one another's eyes. Eventually she starts to speak. Her voice is rich and full, softly accented and beautiful.

"You are the feminine principle of the Divine. You have descended and become imprisoned into matter. You are here now, in this body, to become liberated and to redeem not only yourself, but of all your sparks that are lost in darkness.

The One God became Two. The one original thought created a response called Wisdom. That is how you came into being. But it is true as well to say that you existed in the original one God, the Nameless One.

"In your naturalness you desired to create a reflection of the highest heaven and went about doing this alone, without the concurrence of your consort. Your thought became a singular creation, and then a veil came into being between the highest heaven and the lower regions, or aeons. The light of your thought cast a shadow—not substance, not life—but a shadow of thought. This shadow realized that there was something stronger than itself and then it became envious. Envy was born, permeating all the worlds and regions below the highest heaven. But that envy was an abortion, an excretion without essence and devoid of Divine spirit.

"The hatred and envy were cast into a part of the chaos, and matter came into being. From this origin of matter, the Demiurge, your son, came into his realm of power. You sensed that this spiritless demiurge may attempt to rule over matter. And with that thought came the birth, because at the same time, a great being came out of the waters with much authority within it. Yet it was ignorant of its origins. You originally called him the accursed god, because he made the visible world and kept humanity separate from knowledge."

Pythia pauses and looks at me with penetrating compassion. She smooths the hair back from my forehead with soft murmurs. "I know this is not easy, my love, but you must listen and understand." I nod mutely, and she continues.

"When you saw all that was born from your actions, you were sorely troubled. In the fierceness of your love and compassion you abandoned the Fullness and came into the world of matter to breathe life into the depths of the abyss. Through his word, the demiurge had created worlds where he ruled and controlled: heavens and earth, orders and hierarchies in his heavens. He was arrogant in his creation and caused all creatures to praise him saying, "I am the only God. No other exists before me." In your previous encounters with him you would do battle with him, trying to reveal the real nature of things. There have been so many times that you have cried out, "You lie, Samael!"

She stops, looking directly into my eyes. I can't hide the bombshell that has just exploded inside my own heart.

"Samael? Samael? My Samael?" I ask her.

"Yes" she whispers. "*Your* Samael"

"But, how? I mean, is he ... Oh God!" I freeze in terror with the implications of what this might mean.

She squeezes my hand, indicating there is more to share.

"Samael means *god of the blind* and that is what he is. In the world of matter you were promptly set upon by the archons, the rulers of his world, who defiled you and in their rage, rendered you blind. You cried out in despair and regret at the tragedy you had caused to exist and suffered bitterly from your separation of the Nameless One. The cry of your voice spanned countless universes searching to be heard by the most High. In your voice, my dear, humanity can hear its own blindness and ignorance reaching to be touched by the divine Presence.

"The Nameless One, in his love for his own feminine self, has sent into the world of matter a redeemer, a reflection of his own Self, whom we call the Logos. The Logos will restore your sight and reunite with you. In your reunion, the lost sparks of humanity can also be made whole and all will be reunited with the Most High."

"I've met him! I have dreamt about him already – the Logos I mean!" I excitedly blurt out.

"I know Sophia. I saw Him coming. He has been waiting for so long on the edges of your psyche, waiting patiently for you to reach out to him." Her eyes search mine, looking, looking all over for *something*, some connection, some glimmer of recognition perhaps?

I am not sure whether she finds it, as all I can feel in this moment is the heaving weight of universal grief. I am almost choking with regret and I'm filled with a sense of shame that threatens vanquish me.

"Sophia." Pythia's eyes bore into my soul. "You are the Holy Sophia, the element that has chosen out of love and compassion to dwell in darkness. You are the Holy Presence, which has been defiled and spurned by many. Yet it is this Presence that spurs us on towards the wholeness against all odds. It is your voice, which is also our own, that cries out from the depths of ignorance and alienation and manages to reach the Most High God.

"Sophia, this call creates a bridge across the stars that move within the space that is us; this call permits the Divine Bridegroom to extend his healing touch and with a kiss that is bathed in tears, He turns our blindness into sight. You are the Consecration and the Communion, and when you wed once again to the Logos, we will all be called to the wedding feast of celebration. For at that moment, you shall lift the veils that cloaked your divinity, revealing the Bride and Bridegroom, face to face, and sealed by the bridge to the Most High. And everything and everyone shall have safe passage to the Light."

Between gasps of air I ask, "What about Samael? What becomes of him?" Shaking with emotion I wait for what seems like eternity for the answer.

"That is something I don't know, because it is something that has not yet been decided. What becomes of Samael will be a choice that he alone has to take. You will open the bridge for him. Whether he accepts his place, fully redeemed and in servitude to the Light— is up to him."

As she speaks, I notice that everything is shape shifting into a melting mélange of light and color. I feel myself entering a whirlpool of liquid light, as gossamer thin wisps of color emerge between us. Particles of light dance in front of my face.

But Pythia has turned away. She seems to be looking beyond into a vague and unknown distance. Mesmerized, I watch how a single, solitary tear falls from her eye in slow motion. My heart quickens, sensing that my time here is drawing to a close. I look up at her, silently pleading to stay. *I don't want to leave you*, I silently cry. Plumes of vaporous mist slowly rise up and form the most exquisite panoply of celestial light. I feel torn; part of me wishes that I could stay here forever, while another part graciously accepts what has already been given, and swells in adoration.

Here in Pythia's presence I feel totally reborn. My purpose is rekindled, restored and elevated to the highest imaginable beauty. Yet I must leave. Our fingers begin to disentangle, and I turn once again to see her perfect teardrop slowly nearing the ground. I watch in a haze as I am drawn backwards, back towards the physical realm, where my body is waiting for me in the worn leather armchair. Just before the teardrop explodes into shards of liquid light, she looks up, but the face I see is not hers—instead, it is my own.

Chapter 16

Beloved Reunion

Everything feels different. After sleeping the best part of seventy-two hours, I feel restored and ready to explore. The great weight has lifted from my shoulders and I feel like myself again. I need to get out of these jeans and sweatshirt and luxuriate in a long hot bath. I want to look beautiful. I need to remember what that feels like again. I pull the hair band from my hair, loosening my scarlet curls from their permanent three-month topknot. I have almost forgotten what I look like with my hair down. I peer in the mirror as I turn my head from side to side, realizing that the period of deadness has come to an end. In its place is the desire to kick back, relax and have some fun.

I have decided to actually leave the house for the first time since I got here! I am going to check out the local Sunday market in Puivert, remembering that Pythia said it was a "must see." She described it to me as a glorious mélange of spontaneous bohemian performance and organic local produce. A breath of fresh air is just what I need! It's going to be fun, and yet, I feel kind of silly—a little bit shy—as if I am going to meet someone there. I giggle to myself like a blushing sixteen-year-old schoolgirl being admired by the boys, embarrassed and at the same time loving it. I brush the thought aside, but still it feels *so* good to imagine …

I pull everything out of my suitcase, examining all the clothes I packed. I decide on the buttercup yellow strapless floor length dress, with my chocolate leather hand-made tribal gypsy boots— gorgeous knee high boots that lace together like a corset up my shinbone. They are incredibly sexy and act as a sure fire aphrodisiac every time I wear them, for both myself and any unsuspecting onlooker.

After spending an obscene amount of time in the bathroom, I emerge looking totally transformed. I feel incredible: truly beautiful with a softness that radiates out around me. I feel young and *untouched*. As I open up the front door, I become bathed in sunrays. Joyfully, I inhale the glorious mid morning air. For the first time in three days I set foot outside the house and venture out into the great unknown.

I can feel someone staring at me. The persistent presence of another warms my back, enticing me to look over my shoulder. My heightened instincts quicken, sensing the welcome energy of an ally. Yet in this material world, I am not about to take any chances. For all I know it might be Samael. I must know for sure that I am safe; that my subtle, yet consistent watcher is benevolent.

I merge into the organized chaos of the Sunday market, becoming one with the spectrum of colors, sounds, and countless smells that evocatively entice me with the promise of sensual satisfaction. I reach over a cascading display of plump, blushing apples to peruse an assortment of unsuspecting figs. As the tips of my fingers delicately brush over them, feeling for their ripeness, I become acutely aware of this warm presence touching my back again. I tingle with anticipation. Transformed instantly—my breath quickens. For a moment, I am suspended between two worlds. I imagine not only the innermost taste of the fig once bitten into, but also my own sweet offering in the inevitable moment when my eyes meet those of this other. Even now, the hair tingles on the back of my neck, and the light of remembrance flares quickly in my guarded heart.

My blood pounds with the profound inevitability of this moment. Every second builds upon the next, intensifying the immense attraction that is beginning to engulf me. It tears at my heart as well. A resounding stillness encircles me. I am suspended in the calm before the storm, acutely aware of the hairline gap between aloneness and reunion. My breath echoes inside my chest, and I feel for the right moment to turn around and look into the face of my observer. Seconds spill into minutes as I retrieve parts of me that are already beginning to stray into futuristic thinking.

Be here now, in this moment—this moment between space and time, and see me.

My eyes widen in wonder and I catch my breath. Where did these words come from? Are they my own thoughts, or the voice of my beholder? My blood is intoxicated with this soulful expression, and my face flushes, as I patiently wait for the figs for to become mine through an exchange of currency. Praying that the stallholder will serve me next, I tingle with the ghost of warm breath upon my untouched skin. I feel his presence send me tumbling into the mystery. As I calmly hand over the price of my figs, inside I am thirsting to turn around, to touch the healing infusion of his eyes in mine. I become silent and still, suddenly aware of how very starved I have been, how frozen without the warmth of this penetrating, tender gaze. Grace descends as I lower my eyes, bowing to the sacredness of this holy moment.

For so long, my only companions have been the voices of fear and doubt, the opiate of the masses, who mocked my every twist and turn as I sought him. They hounded me the moment I fell to this "God forsaken" place, ridiculing my prayers, scoffing at my faith in Him. Memories surface, past fragments of forgotten times in a crazy kaleidoscope eons long. Every possible future rises and falls in whispered surrender as a warm-blooded silence sweeps through me. From the tumultuous core of my being, an ever faithful and innocent sentence forms, renewing a light within that had almost diminished.

Logos—is it you?

The tender purity of my question scrapes against the hardened walls of my sacred heart. I had not been brave enough to think this thought after my world grew dark. After all, years of prayers had piled up to protect me from the pain when he did not come. Many had imagined that I lost my sight. But I hadn't. I had simply closed my eyes to a world that could not bear Him.

I am pulled back into the present moment by the delicate weight of those eyes sweetly caressing my form, soaking in my every feature. I feel exposed—naked. No, no it isn't that! Oh God. I feel seen, met, and recognized. This realization clamors at the edge of my soul. *There is only one that knows me.* The familiar sound of my own voice startles me. These words burn at my throat as a strange bittersweet longing crawls up inside my ribs. My heart begins to thunder, creating a visible pulse between my breasts. The almighty power of Love awakens in me, and erupts from its slumber. This Love is so merciful, pure and eternal, that at times in the past, its very innocence was a weight upon my shoulders.

For the first time in a long, long while, I open myself to beauty, like a rose unfurling in the sun. Slowly I turn around to meet the One I had been looking for my entire life. Sunlight dances on his face, sending delicate wisps of golden amber across his eyes. For a moment I cannot see the fullness of his features, yet I receive an impression of lasting kindness. His fingers reach for mine, offering me steadiness in my suddenly swirling world. I feel overwhelmed, flooded with spiraling sensations, and yet so eager, so hopelessly embracing the entirety of this heavenly moment.

I see his face. The clearest eyes that I have ever seen—eyes that have been imprinted into my heart since the beginning of time—look back into mine. They are the eyes of an angel, loving and reassuring. They are the very eyes that were once lost and longed for, and here they are—open and alive, embodied and real. My heart reaches like a bamboo flute for the soaring tones of love, as I tenderly move forward to touch him. The golden light fills my outstretched hand, drenching my thirsty eyes. Our hearts join in a harmony of prayer as every thought and feeling turns to the Divine, and my universe fills with peace.

"My Love, do you remember me?"

He holds my face with both his hands. His eyes search mine for an answer, spoken or silent. His resonant voice vibrates through me like a warm fragrant breath, carrying the voice of gods, men and angels. This frequency of sound undoes me, and matches the note of my own soul.

My answer is a single tear, a brilliant jewel of light that caresses my face, and falls into his awaiting fingertips.

Seconds become minutes, possibly hours, even days. The lively chaos of the market place fades from my awareness. Once known and familiar reference points like time and space just dissolve. I know nothing, nor do I need to. My only desire is to be here and now with him for as long as possible, to absorb his presence, to drink from his mouth, to taste from his fingers.

Before me stands a man basked in kindness, carrying the light of a living sun. His open heart beams a love so radiant and boundless that he encircles me and wraps me in invisible arms. Beside him is the most handsome wolfhound. Standing proud and loving, he watches with eyes that are not from this world. Together, they are angels. Truly, the presence of them soothes my ancient aching aloneness. I am transfixed, swaying between faith and doubt.

The man's face seems to carry the bloodline of the gypsies. Full-bodied, fair, shoulder length hair glints with reddish tones as the sunlight frames his silhouette. His eyes remind me of cobalt blue pools glistening with compassion. Love visibly rises inside of him and shines from those eyes. His body is strong but gentle, clothed in blue jeans and a plum cotton collarless shirt, sleeves rolled up to reveal bronzed muscular forearms. I notice his hands. His fingers are elongated and beautifully kept; these hands feel the joy of his work. They are an artist's hands. I look down and notice tiny droplets of paint on his sandals, and my hunch is confirmed.

Even though I know it is *him*, I just can't understand how he appears inside this human body. I never once imagined that he could physically incarnate on Earth, and yet here *I* am, wrapped within a body of flesh, walking towards the nearest café with *him*—my eternal Beloved, brother and best friend. His hand reaches for mine, his thumb brushing against the inside of my wrist. My heart swoons in response, as we walk together, *Logos* at my right and his wolf at my left. I can't even think. My mind half attempts to formulate questions, but it is impossible. So, I just continue to breathe, not wishing to miss a blessed moment of our time together.

We find a quiet table on the terrace of a café. Shabby but chic, this quirky little hangout offers us the much-needed privacy that we crave. We pull out two rustic chairs with wobbly legs, and sit like ordinary people at a wooden table. His wolf goes underneath the table and rests at his feet. Smiling at the novelty of it all, we reach for each other's hands across the table, our fingers and eyes eager to discover, caress, stroke and drink from the essence of the other. It has been so long, this treacherous journey of separation! Every now and again I get to see another face beyond his, a face that stares back at me with ineffable beauty. This visage is so pure and holy, that I look away in shame.

Composing myself I return to the *Logos*, laughing inwardly at our awkwardness. We are unsure how to behave, or what to speak of. So in this innocence, we simply stare into one another's eyes, and our hands squeeze messages of love in a language we instantly recognize.

A waitress comes to take our order. Do I even see her? I am completely unable to peel my eyes away from him, in case I miss some expression of his beauty that I would come to depend upon when the aloneness returned. While we sit here, cocooned within this vibrant bohemian café, he takes the initiative and begins to speak. He slowly explains that he is the one whom I have been seeing in my visions and dreams and that his name is Logos. He pauses, making sure I am taking in every thing that he says.

I nod at him to continue. *I am with you so far.*

He explains that he doesn't know how it happened, but only hours ago he found himself inside this human body. He tells me that a greater force is orchestrating this whole process and that this being is known as the Nameless One.

"He is the one who sent me forth, to find you," he says softly.

"What do you mean, find me?"

He takes a deep breath and looks down into his lap, seeming to search for something. I silently watch as his shoulders rise and fall like a colossal ocean. He lifts his eyes, revealing a presence that astounds me. Everything grows silent as the noise of the café fades and I am transported into a world where only we exist.

"I am only a reflection of Him. I am a messenger. The *Logos*. The word of God."

"No, no, you are more than that," I cry. "You are my beloved, my liberator. You exist—you are here—you are real!"

"Sophia, I am light cloaked in flesh for only a limited time. I am here only long enough to find you," he whispers. "Only long enough to create the bridge to the Most High."

My heart explodes like the last remaining star in existence. What was holy rapture only a moment ago, has now been crushed underfoot by the cruelest monster imaginable.

His hand tightens on mine. "Since I was created all I have ever known is you. Your face, your voice, your name—everything about you enchants me. I have been created *only* to find you. Once I have found you, simultaneously the bridge opens up between you and the Nameless One, and separation ends."

Hot tears stream down my face as the wolf gets up and places his head upon my lap. His big brown eyes burrow into mine sending waves of virtuous strength and protection.

"My essence is suffused with a burning light that propels me towards you, but *only* when you reach for me. When you call, I am there, and when I am there—you are in silent communion with … Him. This is how you shall return—by filling yourself with Him. It is *through* him that I exist. I am the part of God that can *travel*. The Nameless One is the effulgent presence of God that holds open the heavens with his Light. If He were to leave, all of creation both manifest and unmanifest would implode."

I reluctantly nod. Utterly broken-hearted that this man before me wasn't going to stay, I feel weak and shaky. I know that in some uncertain time I will have to let go of these comforting hands. My soul feels as if it is sliding down a cheese grater. It is almost unbearable—but somehow I know I have to go on.

The Logos holds me up with his eyes. "For eons I have waited, silently in the space between worlds. I was waiting for you to cry out for my help, to say that you needed me, and that without me you were lost. I too, have felt the same way … that the meaning of my life only becomes fulfilled the moment I meet you."

The silence thickens. I get the feeling that two people are speaking to me. I begin to drift away, overloaded with the amount of light coursing through my body. Somewhere, however, a part of me is still listening. He speaks of being thrust into life by a consistent and ever-growing desire, a compulsion and need to find me. He speaks of hurtling through spheres of light, through dimensional realms of existence in order to find me. He tells me that he had no idea where he was going, but he was drawn by a deep, primordial sense of knowing, which simply had to be obeyed.

He says that finding me has resulted in him becoming a bridge—a bridge of living light that stretches all the way towards the Nameless One. His brilliant eyes look right into mine, and he affirms that the path is now open for our return to the Pleroma. With warm urgency, he reminds me that it is the beauty of our love reunited that lights the way for all who can see.

"*Logos*, what about the rest of us, all the human souls? I can't leave them behind," I whisper. "We all must go together!"

He stares me for a long time, a very long time as his eyes search mine. Eventually he moves by brushing the tears from my cheeks with the back of his hand. "Is this your choice, then? You wish to remain here until every single human soul has been retrieved by you?"

Something primeval stirs within me. "Yes" I reply.

With the delivery of that one word we stand up and grab one another, holding on for dear life. An alchemical elixir of grief, sorrow, grace, love and profound understanding surges through our one body, heart and soul. Without knowing it, our Divine Love showers redemptive seed into the hearts of humanity, and the Bridge of Light grows even stronger.

The rest of this miraculous afternoon is spent piecing the puzzle back together. I have so many questions that beg for answers, yet many times he is unable to answer them, and his face remains silent in compassion. I have a feeling that inside he knows what is really happening, and the cross that he has to bear is one of helplessness. Every now and again he hints that I hold the eventual outcome in my hands: that I hold the keys to fulfilling this journey. When he speaks in this way, he looks so intently at me, and he pauses to hang weight on what he is saying.

"You can only do this Sophia, if you allow my Light to fill you. It is together that we can accomplish this. Together, Thy will shall be done".

As the sun drops towards the horizon, the vibrant world diminishes all around us, revealing a hushed and unwanted feeling that our time together is only temporary.

"Sophia. I am so close to you now, although I have to remain at a distance. I am not able to materialize on Earth for very long, otherwise I too could undergo the same fate as yourself."

My heart burns with his words. I know that he speaks the truth, yet I do not want to believe. My mind runs in circles searching for answers. But it is my angry fire that reaches him first.

"Do you know what its like to feel abandoned? I want to know if *you* are prepared to live in this world, despite its harsh need to change you. I want to know if *you* can look back with firm eyes and say—*this* is where I stand! I want to know if you can melt into the fierce heat of living, *even* as you cleave to the center of your longing. I want to know if you are willing to live, day by day, with the consequences of our love *despite* the sense of bitter passion that torments you of your sure defeat!"

My eyes glare at him, filling with tears of certain glory. I'm exuberant from voicing my deepest victory cry. Yet I am still reeling from the unwavering swathes of pure love and redemption that continue to pour through his face.

Gently, he repeats, "Sophia, I know what you have gone through. But do not hold too tightly to your experiences. You have plunged into the deepest hells and faced the darkened recesses of creation, but now it is time to complete the full cycle and ascend.

Every second, every moment, relies on you. It you want this—just let my Light touch you."

Heavy waves of shame flood through me, darkening my countenance, whispering words of retreat. But I hold still, refusing to succumb to their false protection. I shudder at the enormity of my task. In this incarnation, there are times when I am filled with a sense of hope and glory, and there are times when I am utterly blind to everything. Now seems to be one of those times. Nothing makes sense. Why would I delay my own return? Why would I spend so many hours, days, nights, years—hundreds, thousands, *millions* of years separated from the one I loved most of all?

My heart implodes with sorrow, and yet within the depths of despair there is a light, a flickering wisp of fortitude. I absolutely know that I will go on, and that to even consider that I will accept a different outcome is simply a form of entertainment. There is truly no choice; I was born to do this. Even during the times when I am not sure I am on the right path, I will persevere. If I give up now, I will die.

After this utterly Divine meeting today in the marketplace, I have seen with my own eyes the living proof that this is not a dream.

I AM Sophia.

I have given myself to the depths of matter to bring forth the Light, *His* Light. My love for Him has birthed the shimmering Bridge that now exists.

The sweetness of surrender to this Truth fills me with the spirit of victory. I feel utterly warmed and strengthened as I lift my eyes back to his. His gaze is steadfast, waiting for my return, and his entire being is unwavering in his outpouring of love for me. I realize that I control the abundance of this flow. It is up to me to let go of all resistance, and allow this Light to enter me and restore me fully.

"Hear me Sophia. Your time of preparation is complete. Remember that you are born for this task and that I am with you always. Creation waits for you. You are never alone. To feel abandoned is to deny this Truth." His eyes sink into mine, burning with an intensity that devours all my attention.

"Allow me to love you. Open yourself to receive my devotion. Through our love you shall be fully restored. For I carry the Light of the Nameless One. I *am* He, made manifest. I have been created only to love you with every nuance of my existence."

Fire scorches my eyes, as red-hot tears pour down my face. My expression of shame begs for mercy, pleads for forgiveness, and prays for redemption.

He moves closer, and again brushes the tears from my burning cheeks. "My Love, you are forgiven. You only need to forgive *yourself*. You are the Mother of compassion. You always fulfill your true nature. Only because of the enormity of your love did you fall to earth to save your children. Your fierce compassion knows no other way." His beautiful eyes hold mine. "*I* could never have done this."

I am still not sure. "But what about Samael? I created this loveless monster devoid of Divine Light. Can I ever be forgiven for doing this?" I cry.

His smile irradiates me. "You were forgiven the moment it happened, my Love".

The kindness in his eyes tenderly pulls from within me all illusion, all clinging to the idea that I have done something so terribly wrong. With a shuddering sigh of infinite relief, I realize that I have never betrayed the Nameless One—never betrayed all of our creation. I feel stunned, and innocence begins to bubble up with joy.

"My Queen, I come bearing a message from the Nameless One, the one who awaits you at the end of your crucible. He wants you to know that he bows before you for the glorious rebirth that you have extended to mankind. Thinking of you always, he has been filled with sorrow at the knowledge of what you would come to endure here."

Slowly, slowly, increment-by-increment, the weight and majesty of his words penetrate me. I am brought home to my Self—these words restore billions upon billions of stars, they create and destroy universes. These holy words birth love and forgiveness over and over again in boundless celebration.

I am forgiven. I am Sophia, boundless Mother of compassion.

Hand in hand, we instinctively arise, leaving behind the jovial faces of customers waiting for their evening supper. We walk from the café in the deepening dusk, and wander towards the river. The water sings a song of tumbling, bubbling joy. As darkness falls, our voices become whispers, and every question within me fades. The presence of sacredness embraces us. In the darkness, we let go of the physical world and enter the energetic one.

"It is time. Soon I shall have to leave you." The voice of the *Logos* enters the dark peaceful silence. "Come closer my Beloved, for I shall pass the spirit into you the way it was passed into me." He invites me to lean in, inches from his beautiful face. "I am your son, brother, husband and father. When you drink from my mouth you will become like me, I myself shall become you, and the hidden things will be revealed to you. Receive me fully and completely. Then together, little by little, we shall restore your Light."

These words of the Logos unlock something within me, something so terribly ancient and buried that I gasp at its depth. I close my eyes and feel into the great abyss. Something exquisitely tender, and yet fiercely charged, awakens within me.

In the darkness I sense him coming very close. Then his resonant warm mouth touches my full and expectant lips. He holds my face in his hands with utter strength. This energy is electrifyingly intense and thunderously silent. My blood swoons and surges through my body, awakening vast and countless memories, visions, and dreams. Oh, how I had fervently prayed for this moment! In utter joy, I surrender. I open my mouth to receive his holy breath. He inhales deeply, and releases his breath into my mouth. His exhalation lasts forever. Time ceases to exist. The world emerges out of the void and expands—universes spring into form and die.

I know none of that, yet I become a living knowing, beyond all knowing. Nothing is left of what I called me. I simply resound with the sound *I Am*.

Suddenly I open my eyes, and I, Sophia, am alone. Yet I know I will see him again, and that his living Spirit is now inside of me forever.

Chapter 17

Own the Throne

I walk slowly back to the house. Everything is different. I see more. I *feel* more. I hear more. I feel wide open and *spaced out* and I do not know whether to laugh or cry. I feel huge, like a giant: an enormous being that walks the earth filled with the heat of a thousand suns. I feel like I am going to explode into a trillion, million pieces when in actual fact the reverse is true. All the pieces are integrating. I grab the wall with one hand and hold my womb with the other as I double over in ecstatic gratitude.

"My babies, my children are returning," I whisper. When I hear these words I weep so profoundly, as a powerful wave of love cleaves open my chest. *Oh Nameless One, my beloved Light of Lights, thank you for finding me and filling me with your love. I ecstatically burn with rapture as each and every one of our children returns to us!* I gasp and reel for breath while laughing at the same time like a lunatic. As more and more souls return, my ecstasy becomes deeper, my love grows wider.

I don't even notice that I'm outside in a public place; nothing this trivial matters anymore. I do not fully belong to the human race any longer. I am far, far away from all kinds of human conditioning and the myriad ways of trying to fit in. I laugh madly, wildly, freely, as every ounce of social control I once had pours between my fingers. Torrents of love, freedom and truth radiate from my center and consume whoever I thought I was.

I knew this would happen. The Logos had already forewarned me, explaining that every soul I ever co-created would reconnect with me, like a reverse birthing process. He said that within minutes of our kiss, the burning flame of our union would send out a beacon so tremendous, so bright, so infused with majestic light that everyone everywhere would see it, feel it and know that we have reunited.

Just a fraction of time before his lips met mine he had whispered, "Sophia, you have to understand that everyone will sense our reunion, *everyone*. When we do this we will draw infinite attention to ourselves and to our whereabouts. Every living being shall feel this. And this includes Samael and all the forces working for him. You will never go un-noticed after this point. Do you understand?"

And I had nodded in compliance, burning for his sacred breath. I dream the kiss all over again and swoon with elation.

I glimpse Maison Rouge up ahead and have never felt so grateful. Slowly I edge my way towards the front door, unlock it, push it open and let myself in. The moment the door closes I breathe a huge sigh of relief as I drop my purse to the floor.

In my heightened state I am suddenly aware that someone has been here.

No, someone is *still* here. Like a warm vapour made of information particles, I pick up exactly where the source of this presence is coming from—the kitchen. *It's a woman. She moved very quickly; she didn't want to be seen. She has left something here for me to find and she is still watching.*

Sure enough, waiting for me on the kitchen table is a large wicker hamper with a single red rose strewn poetically over the top. *Pythia!* As I get closer I can see the corner of something cream-colored peeking out from underneath the rose. It looks like a letter that has been written centuries ago. I examine the battered and stained envelope. *This looks as if it is something that has been passed down throughout the generations!* My curiosity is piqued. The words, *"To Sophia"* written in blood red calligraphy are cracked, blistered, and even peeling off in some places the moment my fingers touch them.

Mmm, this was written centuries ago ... I open the envelope carefully and unfold the letter. A heavenly burst of light irradiates my face, saturating me in aromas so deliciously familiar. Rose, lavender and musk. New emotions swell in chest as I bring the letter to my nostrils and inhale gently. I get all choked up, imagining for a second that Pythia is my mother, my real mother—my Heavenly Mother. This letter is touching something inside of me that I can't quite put my finger on, *yet.* I know for a fact that I have handled this letter before. I feel as if I have written it to *myself.*

And then the penny drops ... or rather, smashes into smithereens.

Pythia is an aspect of me...

Truth rises within me, causing the hairs on my arms to quiver in bliss and confirm my revelation. I close my eyes as gnosis claims me. An arc of flame gracefully undulates out from the velvety darkness. A fire of gold, liquid in flow, space in substance, unfolds and pulls me in. A sea of glass rolls open like an unfurling magic carpet made from oceans of light. Flecks of liquid fire course through this magnificence. Angels with wings on their faces and thousands of eyes peer at me, convulsing me in orgasmic shivers as countless realizations pour into my mind. Pieces of the puzzle elegantly fall into place leaving me staggering on the expanding edge of who I think I was, and who I Am.

Delirious with awe, I fall back into an awaiting chair, transfixed by the dancing particles of light emerging before me. To my astonishment, I realise that everything I can see and feel on the inside is now forming on the outside! The entire lightshow of my inner world is now appearing in plain sight right in the middle of the kitchen. The gap between the worlds is thinning. Again, I remember the Logos telling me this would happen: that the inner would become the outer, and the outer would become the inner. And, he said, at that moment the bridge to the Most High would be open.

I grip the edge of my seat as the transmission soaks itself into my body rendering me speechless and teeming with life. Drenched and filled with wonder, I look back down at the letter, trying my hardest to read who wrote it. Through a kaleidoscope of glistening tears I witness how the first three letters of the name slowly transfigure into another.

PYTHIA SOPHIA

I stare at the word, expecting another change, but nothing happens. My mind attempts to formulate a sentence and immediately gives up. I glance up at the holographic lightshow that fills the kitchen, unfazed at this point by this breach in "reality."

Slowly, a cold clamouring loneliness encircles me. Because ... if I am Pythia, then I am truly alone. I cry out with the loss of a dear friend, wailing freely into my hands as I rock back and forth, knowing paradoxically that she is inside of me, because she *is* me. *Oh my god this is so crazy!* I wail in loss and loneliness at this new discovery, and then I hear her voice—my voice—say, "Alone and All One. Both the same." I can't help smiling wanly. And then the voice of the *Logos* penetrates me, forming a soothing patina over this internal struggle.

At first you will swing between human and divine realities. Your emotional body will struggle with letting go as your human ego thins and eventually transforms back into pure light. What has been done cannot be undone. I am with you always.

His words glisten with living presence, ravishing every nuance of my being—both human and divine. As His words fill me, I become bathed in an otherworldly glow. His spoken breath is like a canopy of verdant radiance; and I blossom and bloom into ever escalating extensions of love. Gratitude oozes out of me into the fullness of creation as I bask once again in the Logos' magnificence, and in my own ability to do this.

I return to the letter. *By the time you read these words, you will have realized that that your 'helper' is in fact you. The name "Pythia" means prophetess in Greek. It was the name given to the Oracle of Delphi, the one who transmitted the great prophecies— hence the reason why you named the Oracle Pythia after this prophetess aspect of yourself.*

I look up momentarily, allowing the words to sink in. My mind feels incapable of receiving all this information, yet my heart aches with nostalgia for all time that has elapsed between now and *then* ... I intrepidly wander back through my awakening memories, carefully treading on the sacred ground where aspects of myself are waiting. Like a silent movie, I watch at a distance all the roles I have played since the beginning of time. I see all the souls I have loved and cared for, and how, over the duration of these years I have steadily prepared to open the return to the Pleroma.

Smiling softly to myself I gaze out the window, realizing there is nothing I would change about my existence—every moment lived has been such a blessing. I am far from understanding where all this is going, but in this NOW moment I am filled with gratitude with all that has been.

I turn my attention back to the letter. *What you are about to read could have a detrimental effect on you. Allow yourself to read the words slowly, taking in what you can as smoothly and calmly as possible. You have to be incessantly vigilant at a time like this! Now more than ever, you need to know that when you focus excessive attention on the dominion of darkness and ignorance in the world, it causes the remains of your ego to get caught up again in the trap, and so the game of attachment and aversion continues in full swing. This is a trick of the same ignorance and darkness that seeks to compromise your faith, shatter your hope, and extinguish your love! As you know by now, this darkness is Samael. He is the Master of Manipulation—an interwoven snare of anger and fear that seizes the human soul until all light within it slowly diminishes and becomes his.*

When you focus too much upon the darkness it becomes all you think and talk about. You think you are doing good by bringing awareness of the darkness and its sadistic grip on people's lives, but even this very simple act invokes the very powers you are attempting to transform. Inadvertently you will become a channel for the dark forces through your obsessive aversion. In doing so, you will end up discouraged and hopeless, or worse, lost in the violence of radical fundamentalism that believes in purging evil by way of a "holy war." Through this form of extreme aversion, you will become the very evil you propose to banish from the face of the earth. So take care.

The greatest thing you can do right now is to cleave to the highest aspects of Love in action! Do not lose sight of the Nameless One for one second! Bond yourself to the highest echelons of the supernal Light. Act as a fearless midwife to your own Self—armed and aligned with the tremendous self-transfiguring force of Love!

I take a deep breath and continue. *Earth is in a period known as the End of Days. This is a time when you will decide whether the Earth will rebirth herself or cease to be. The escalating darkness is preparing to completely engulf Earth and all her resources (including human souls) by squeezing the life force out of this planet and claiming it for its own purposes. This is precisely why you are here now in this moment, and reading these words!*

This letter is a final reminder to yourself. It was written by yourself in the past for you now, in the future present. This has never happened before, but it was foreseen.

The masses do not know this is happening because the darkness is purposefully withholding all information. Samael will create something called "The Demiurge." This is what he is destined to do. I don't know what shape and form this will take, but it will become something of a drug to the people, something they become addicted to. The demiurge will become a powerful distraction that

siphons the free will from souls, leaving Samael free to rape and
pillage every resource he sees fit.

My heart is pounding. I recognize everything that is written. A
wave of nausea grips my stomach because *Demiurge* is the name
of Samael's company, a virtual reality worldwide web—*a drug to*
the people. I groan out loud as I rush towards the terrace before
violently throwing up outside. I remember how he would gloat
about giving people a 'second life,' one far better than the pathetic
real world. A place where every fantasy could become fulfilled,
every dream lived, and every wish granted—a place so captivating
that they would never want to come back.

I vomit again. I feel disgusted with myself for not realizing
sooner that he was creating such a monster. Yet I must forgive the
past and act now—with Love. I get a cool drink of water in the
kitchen and calm my trembling stomach. I keep reminding myself
that I can do this, and that I was born to do this.

After some time I return to the letter. *The demiurge will have*
within its nature seven rulers known as "Archons." These are the
offspring of Samael.

"Offspring? How on earth did he do that?" I cry aloud in
disbelief. Sickly fascinated, I keep reading.

The archons are channels of klippotic force, the greatest
agencies of darkness. You may recognize them as Wrath, Lust,
Greed, Sloth, Envy, Pride and Gluttony. They are also known as
the Seven Deadly Sins. As the End of Days draws near, a great influx
of souls will incarnate, along with a deluge of spiritual power. All
that is in this world that is bound up in ignorance, dualism and the
illusion of separation shall become amplified. Yet this is for the
good of all. The influx of spiritual power will be a torrent of both

light and darkness, birthing the potential for great good and great beauty, as well as the potential for great evil and great horror.

The result will be a huge acceleration in consciousness, an acceleration of creative evolution in the world, which shall cause something of an evolutionary crisis, one that the whole world and all its inhabitants shall have to face. Yet the awakening of this fiery intelligence in humanity shall give access to greater and greater power, and to the potential of a fully developed divine human consciousness on every level! It will affect everything: the mind, the body and the spirit. It will require a great maturity and responsibility to chose this divine human possibility. Some will be ready; some will be afraid.

Ready or not, this acceleration shall happen regardless, and the question is, will humanity be able to integrate the great power of the Divine and Supernal Being pouring into it? Namely, you.

I take a shaky breath, then a deeper, fuller one. I'm integrating like hell. Namely, you—which is to say, me. After a shiver of panic, the *Logos* sustains me from within as I accept and remember.

Going back to the letter, I read again. *Namely, you.*

"Yes," I say, and the Light within brightens even more with my returning radiance and power.

What is currently standing in your way is the demiurge. While this thing is running, Samael stands to gain all of the light you are intending to bring to earth. If humanity is unaware of what is happening, in its current state it will only generate more and more darkness, as people become lost and bound to the demiurge. The demiurge is managed and controlled by the seven Archons, the seven lords that stand between the human race and the Nameless One. If you can bring the power behind the demiurge down by facing each and every Archon and showing them that they too depend on your light to evolve—you stand a chance.

I exhale deeply, imagining what this might look like, wondering how I could do this. I feel inconceivably heavy. *You have already met these archons. You met them soon after descending to Earth. They encircled you almost right away, taunting and humiliating you, stealing your light and rendering you blind. For eons you were lost in the hell realms, left to wander the infinite horizons of exile. You did not know where you were, but slowly, slowly you began to remember the Light. This remembrance brought forth a great soul —Yeshua Ben Yosef, more commonly known as Jesus Christ. His love for you gave Him the strength to endure the cross in order to reach you in the hells ... and set you free.*

I close my eyes and I am immediately transported back to that time. I see myself wandering in rags throughout a barren death-filled valley. I am shielding my heart, desperately trying to protect the last filament of light that I have. I have hidden it, keeping it safe from the ones who despise me. All of a sudden, from out of nowhere, I feel another's breath upon me and my diminishing, flickering flame is abruptly extinguished. Horrified I look up to see who has cruelly taken from me my last remnant of hope.

Yet in that split second I see the apparition of man with His hand outstretched, beckoning me to come with Him. I notice the hand is bleeding from a wound in the center of His palm. "Come with me if you want to live," He whispers. A ring of glowing angels, clothed in auras of magnificence, shod in raiment's of finest light, adorned with mantles of stars and sceptres of spiralling galaxies, stands before me. Enormous power, celestial power, is contained in their forms, a power so great I want to sink to my knees in a cry of wonder. But He will not let me. Instead He lifts me up, up out of the hells, as showers of celestial hues burst into my consciousness.

When we finally stop, He turns towards me. His face is shining, beaming rays of radiance through me. Drops of light glisten on His brow; ripples of living light emanate from His gleaming countenance. A wave of humility and indestructible knowing courses through me. Wordlessly, He turns around, trailing wakes of stardust behind Him. I want to follow. But He bids me "Not yet."

"Oh Beloved *Logos*, that was you wasn't it?" I whisper. I do not need the answer. I already know.

I turn over the final page of the letter. *You may be feeling that Samael's plan seems almost indestructible. But there is one thing he did not count on, and that is your awakening. He did not foresee that you would ever fully remember who you are, let alone actively partake in your own almighty rebirth, and he certainly did not account for the Logos being part of it too. Together you are the key to his great undoing.*

However, the moment Logos and you recognize one another and come together for the transference of breath, there will be an equal and opposing response from Samael. His response will be swift, deadly and wide-scale. He will attempt to dissuade you by threatening to harm all life.

Fear ripples through me as I imagine the extent of what Samael is capable of.

You must always remember that what you are about to experience has the possibility of being used for the highest good. Even Samael and the archons have the possibility of returning back to the fullness and relinquishing all ignorance and separation. After all, this is exactly as you envisioned it. You are the Queen of

Heaven—and now is the time for you to Own the Throne. Reclaim your sovereignty, restore your nobility and take back what is rightfully yours.

Yours Eternally,
Sophia

I sink back into the chair as the letter slips through my fingers onto the floor. Before I have time to collect my thoughts, my cell phone starts ringing. I take it out from my pocket and see that my mother is calling.

"Hey Mom, how you doing, is everything okay?" I ask in a voice that hopefully resembles my own.

"Darling, have you seen the news," she gasps.

"No, why what's happening?" I ask.

"There has been an explosion at a nuclear power plant in the Bay Area and thousands have died. Sophia, radioactive waste is leaking out into the ocean and no one can stop it. It is terrible—sheer mayhem! The authorities are trying to evacuate the people but it's chaos! Young people are looting, animals are dying, the forests are burning and no one knows to what extent the radiation could spread." Her tears choke her voice and prevent her from speaking further.

"Mom, stay on the phone. Let me just get online to see the news," I answer. I am doing my best to stay calm and focused. The letter is proving all too true.

I open up my Mac and type in CNN latest news. The screen reveals an escalating carnage of disaster. Fires are exploding before my eyes as I watch the live coverage. People are running and screaming, telling the news crew to drop everything and leave. CNN was a barrage of high scale alerts and warnings to avoid the area. *Oh my God.* I have a sinking feeling. I need to know exactly what caused this to happen.

"Mom, I'm still here. Do you know how this happened? What is being said?" I ask.

Between sobs she says that a satellite fell to earth and crashed into the nuclear reactor. Sickness returns to my stomach. I know what she will say next.

"That's why I called, Sophia. It was Samael's company that caused the satellite to crash!" She starts crying again. "I don't know how it happened, but it was something to do with uploading too much data. Their systems, or computers or whatever, have grown so large that they sent out a radio wave or a pulse or a something and it interfered with the satellite system. We are being told that maybe even more will fall in the coming hours!"

I breathe rapidly as I catch a glimpse of the letter lying open on the floor. I am utterly horrified at Mom's news, yet I have just been told very precisely that something like this would happen. God help me! *Let the games begin ...*

I draw strength from this sense of inevitability and my own part in it. I am on my mission. I tell my mom to leave LA with my dad and stay with their friends in Toronto. I assure them they will be safe there, and the radiation won't reach that far. I firmly stress that they must leave now, this very day. She calms down as she hears the loving strength in my voice and she promises me they will leave immediately.

Then she adds, "Darling what about you? Are you safe in France? When will you be coming home?"

"Mom, I'm fine. Don't worry about me. Just make sure you and Dad get out of there. I have something here that I have to complete. I'm strong, and I know exactly what I am doing, probably for the first time in my life. Just stay in contact with me, okay? Mom, I have to leave now. I love you and I love Dad. Please tell him for me." We hang up.

I pick up the letter and put it in my back pocket as I realize how much I have already endured, and how unfazed I am at having to endure more. Then I search the Internet for news on the Demiurge. Bingo. In a few seconds I find exactly what I want. The headline reads: *Demiurge's new Paris headquarters. Demiurge has opened their new French headquarters. The new Demiurge office is located at 8 Rue de Londres, Paris—in a new 10,000-square meter office located in a newly refurbished art deco hotel near the St. Lazare Train Station. The costly remodel spared no expense in its lavish decoration and latest technologies ...*

"No surprise there," I snort in disgust. I have read enough. I call for a cab to take me to Carcassonne train station so I can get to Paris. In our last meeting Samael kept remarking how much I have changed. And he's right. I have, and soon he will see exactly how much.

Chapter 18

To the Pleroma

He feels the strong upward beat of leathery wings as He soars through the Bridge Most High towards the Pleroma. The Logos and His Dragon dance and curl like scarlet snakes as they approach the velvet-black beckoning force of a gigantic black hole. Within nano-seconds of entering its field, they are thrust into the event horizon—the point beyond which nothing can escape the black hole's grip. The annihilating orbit weighs in at five million times the mass of the sun, and sends them into an agonizing centrifugal spin.

Through boiling and bulging eyes the Dragon can see a point in front of them where all light is being engulfed. With His remaining strength, the Logos looks back just long enough to see an infinitely energetic flash of light from the outside world containing a pictorial transmission of the entire history of the universe. This is the light that vaporizes everything, but this is the very Light that will free the Logos and his Dragon. On and on they hurl toward the black hole's crushing central singularity. Here all light, matter and life stretch into oblivion and morph into a horizontal ring of swirling mass, which the black hole immediately swallows.

The moment they enter the center, there is an implosion of silence that screams all around them. Absolute stillness forces their surrender. They have reached the end of the black hole, and are nearing the portal of a white one. For a split second they are suspended outside of time and space in the nothingness where there is no breath, no movement, no light, no-thing. In this fraction of existence there is only consciousness. The Logos and his Dragon blink in the emptiness. Then they are savagely accelerated outwards—this time in the opposite direction.

An obliterating blaze of light irradiates their arrival. As they rocket from the center of the white hole, a picture of the entire future of the universe flashes before them. Instead of falling inward, this time-space falls outwards at a speed faster than light. The light of The Logos is being unmercifully expanded at breakneck speed. The pain of extreme openness splices His central pillar of self. They hurtle through the white hole, and there is a third flash of light as they rupture its outer horizon. This time the Celestial Kingdom-Queendom appears before them, shimmering in brilliance. Behind them, the last shards of light glow from the white hole of their emergence.

With no effort, the Logos and his Dragon drift slowly towards the Pleroma. The Divine Light caresses and restores their beings. Slowly and gently they are drawn towards the gates of the Celestial Kingdom. Millions of heavenly eyes peer towards them in wonder, for no one has ever returned to the Pleroma through the black and white holes before.

Awareness returns to The Logos as they spiral into the heavenly waters that surround the Pleroma. Every now and again the gentle waves cause them to nudge into the crystalline forms growing out of the celestial ocean they float upon. Each little touch ripples through the Logos, bringing Him more and more into wakefulness. The crystalline formations bask in every hue imaginable, as they whisper of glories yet to come. They coalesce, to form the shores of the Kingdom-Queendom itself. Ornate leaves of wrought gold and lapis lazuli curl around delicate stems of the softest ruby jasper. Embossed in the swaying silken robes of sapphire, the blue white fires of creation cool into translucent light.

"Stop, who goes there?" A powerful booming voice penetrates the lingering swathes of their dream, shattering all veils and bringing them acutely into the present moment.

"Peter, it is I, the Logos. Open the gates! I must speak with the Nameless One immediately." The Logos speaks with authority, and His Dragon stands proudly behind Him.

"Logos! Good heavens! Is that really you? Come through my Lord, for this is indeed a blessed day! Let me sound the trumpets announcing your return!" Peter hurriedly pulls open the magnificent heavenly gates. The bright call of the trumpets announces over and over again that *the Logos has returned*!

As soon as He enters the Kingdom, the enormity of Love explodes in His heart, causing His dragon to draw back his head and rain down a firestorm of effulgent liquid light. *Home!* The gates of the Pleroma close firmly behind them. The Logos takes a couple of steps and stands still to absorb the divine beauty. A ring of glowing angels clothed in auras of magnificence, shod in raiment's of finest light, adorned with mantles of stars and scepters of spiraling galaxies, stand before Him. Enormous power— Celestial Power—lives in their forms. He sinks to His knees in a cry of wonder before this magnificent power, as showers of celestial colors burst into His consciousness.

One of the angels turns towards Him. Her face shines, beaming rays of radiance through Him. Drops of light glisten on her brow; ripples of living light emanate from Her gleaming countenance. A wave of humility and indestructible knowing courses through the Logos. Wordlessly, She turns around, trailing wakes of stardust behind her. He follows, knowing She will escort Him to the one He desperately must see.

Slowly they walk through the crowd of angels, who extend their fingertips in salutation, to touch Him and show their love. These angels form the third sphere of Heaven, known as the Principalities and Divine messengers of the Nameless One. Their energy is like a divine angelic choir, diffusing the most effervescent and contagious purity.

Beyond them awaits the second sphere of Heaven: the Dominions, Virtues and Powers, known as the Heavenly Governors. These fiery light beings carry out the divine will of the Nameless One and maintain the hierarchies of heaven in true and perfect order. As the Logos approaches, they step back into line extending their feathered wing tips to form a path and to gently stroke the being they love so adoringly.

At last they reach the first sphere of Heaven—the mighty Seraphim, Cherubim, Ophanim and Thrones. Before approaching them, the Logos pauses to bow his head, showing His respect and recognition of nobility. These beings are known as the Hosts of the High Court, and they live directly below the Nameless One. They comprise the Angelic inner circle; they are the very ones who formed the alchemical vessel within which the Logos was created.

They recognize Him immediately, and bring one wing to their hearts while extending the other towards the Throne of God. An incorruptible Light permeates the atmosphere around the Throne. It seeps through the Logos, and gradually dissipates the memories and echoes of what He has recently endured.

The Logos drops to His knees once more to brace Himself for the appearance of the Nameless One. Suddenly, a resounding cry of delight fills the heavens. The Nameless One has seen His Son! He runs down from the great Throne with arms outstretched, and falls upon the Logos, wrapping Him in His arms and kissing His cheeks. The first sphere of Angels swells with adoration and weeps tears of happiness for the reunion of these two Beloveds. The Nameless One orders a robe to be brought for the Logos, and for the great temple gong to be sounded, calling all to a feast, which shall be given in honor of the Logos' safe return.

The Logos melts into the Nameless One's embrace. Their indescribable joy extends into the temple halls, where their divine light and glory is reflected by an immense ocean of glass windows for all existence to see and rejoice in. It is indeed a glorious moment, this precious reunion. The whole of creation ripples with ecstasy. This very moment is felt, everywhere, by *everyone—in all worlds.*

After countless rhapsodies of praise, the Logos draws the Nameless One aside for a private discourse.

"Your Majesty, I have found Sophia, and She is well," He whispers.

"I know Logos; I see and feel everything through your eyes," twinkles the Nameless One.

"Do you know that She has decided to stay until every one of your souls can be saved and returned to the Pleroma?" enquires the Logos.

The Nameless One throws back His head and laughs bountifully. "Ha, of course! That is who She is—the Mother of Mercy," he cries. "This is beautiful—tell me more!" He interlaces His fingers and rests them on His chest, eager to hear the rest of the story.

The Logos is briefly taken aback. He had imagined that the Nameless One would be concerned at the events unfolding on earth and possibly troubled by Sophia's affairs, but this is clearly not the case.

"Well, erm ... do you know about Her son, Samael?" the Logos cautiously asks.

"Of course," the Nameless One replies.

"Are you aware that he has gone on to create the demiurge—" The Logos hesitates for a moment before continuing, "um—and seven archonic forces?"

"Hmmm, seven? Ah yes that's right," the Nameless One confirms.

"And uh ... You are okay with that?' asks the Logos.

"Yes of course. This is exactly how She wanted it." He smiles kindly at the Logos, who is becoming more confused.

"Beloved One. There is something I do not understand. She imagined that you would be distraught with these events. Do you know the demiurge is enslaving human souls and destroying the planet? She is down there all alone and only gradually realizing who She really is and what She might be capable of! " The Logos' voice is rising in distress.

"But She is realizing, yes?" asks the Nameless One.

"Well, yes, but very slowly!" The Logos feels his urgency at the situation rising.

"Wonderful. Really, that is all that matters," replies the Nameless One in a soothing tone. "Come, let's walk and I will explain everything to you." With that, the Nameless One links arms with His Son and together they walk towards the shores of existence.

Sharing silent footsteps, the Logos waits eagerly for His creator to speak. He can feel the delicate presence of the Universe pressing down upon Him, making Him acutely aware of the vastness of the Nameless One's Creation. Wonderstruck, He bows in reverence to the majesty of it all. An arc of flame gracefully undulates out from the velvety darkness. A sea of glass rolls open, an unfurling magic carpet in an ocean of light. Flecks of liquid fire course through this ocean of brilliance, showering sparks of life here and there.

A fluttering mass of wings fills the space for an instant, surrounding and overwhelming Him with their booming gentle power. Space peels back and dissolves into blazing radiance, coruscating cornucopias of colors dazzling, blinding and revealing, all at the same time. The Logos gasps in awe as the ocean of light coalesces its magnificence into a gleaming diamante sphere. A rapt reverie descends upon the Logos, calming Him.

At last, the Nameless One speaks, slowly and thoughtfully. "Logos, everything that is happening on earth is because Sophia wishes to experience it. It is Her nature to firstly know and then embody the whole spectrum of possibility. Sophia is Wisdom. To hold such an authority one must fully embody it. And to embody it, one must experience it." The Nameless One paused and gazed out to the vastness of space.

"I knew at the very beginning that She was destined to take this journey. For this journey *is* the journey of life. She has to know all things by being all things, because... She is all things." The Nameless One smiles at Him, but the Logos still has a burning question.

"Then why did you create me to find Her?" As his words reverberate, a solemn hush suspends them, and peace laps at the shores of the Logos' troubled concerns. Pure silence, cocooned in tender light, swathed in the gentlest of touches, pierces His heart.

"Because I cannot be separate from Her." The Nameless One turns to face Him. "And because—though I know better—she imagined that we were separate."

"So, all of this on earth is unfolding for the fullness of Sophia to be realized," The Logos queries in bewilderment.

"Yes," answers the Nameless One.

"But ... your concern at the beginning—what was that?" The Logos asks insistently. After all, this is a question of His very existence.

"Love. I wished for Her to stay with me, and She had seemingly disappeared," The Nameless One replied.

"*Seemingly* disappeared?" the Logos quizzed. "But I found her *there*!"

"She sent forth Her likeness into the descent of matter, while Her essence remained intact within the realm of the Pleroma," said The Nameless One.

Impaled upon this spear of truth, the Logos staggers back, desperately trying to come to terms with what the Nameless One has said. His heart is gently breaking in a devastating beauty; so devastating as to be terrible, so beautiful that it halts the rest of existence in its tracks. Everything stops. For Sophia is *here*, and She is utterly unspoiled.

The Nameless One sees the Logos' confusion and his sudden awareness. He continues his discourse, explaining that Sophia cannot be separated from Her true self, although She had imagined that She was separate. He tells the Logos how this great unfolding on earth will eventually open the opportunity for all of life to return to its original purity, enhanced with a profound knowing of the whole spectral field of existence. To live is to experience profound darkness *and* profound light.

"You see," he says, "every soul that Sophia births carries a piece of Her inside it. Through that soul, Sophia experiences yet another aspect of life, deepening again her vast and limitless understanding and wisdom. Sophia is in a perpetual state of expansion and contraction—ever growing, ever birthing, and ever dying."

The Nameless One pauses to let that sink in. Then he explains that Samael and the archons also rely upon Sophia for their evolution. He declares it is because of Her that they exist, and it is because of Her that they shall evolve. He reassures the Logos that in time the archons will realize this truth because Sophia will realize it. She will remember that She is their mother, and from that understanding an unshakable love will be reborn and all separation will whither and dissolve.

The Logos listens intently as the Nameless One continues the story: how in the beginning Samael also imagined that he was separate from his mother, and this brought him tremendous pain and suffering. His pain of rejection was so huge that he created a death machine and named it the demiurge. Yet it was also Samael who chose to take Sophia as a wife on Earth. Despite the suffering She caused him, he could not bear to be apart from Her.

Finally, the Nameless One tells the Logos, "My Son, despite

what you have seen on Earth, there is no such thing as evil or sin; there is only ignorance, and true ignorance is ignoring Who you really are. However, it is a matter of time. Eventually all shall return to its right place. It is inevitable—all must return to its original perfection. Yet, my dear Logos, pain and suffering is very real indeed, as you most likely know by now."

The Nameless One looks intently at his Son. "That is why I need you to return to Earth. Go back, and continue to shine your light upon Her, and upon all who ask to receive you. I will inform the guides and guardians of the human souls that you are even closer than before, and that you shall come to every single soul the moment they ask. It is with Sophia's compassion that I say this, because through Her I can feel the enormity of Her love for all souls. She is within all things and She is the Great Mother. This journey of Sophia's must unfold at every level. When the time is right, everyone and everything within all timelines shall collapse into one."

The beginnings of clarity shine a light into the Logos, and with deep compassion He understands the anguish of Sophia. He responds by falling into a deep peace, a rest He has craved, a soft reverent repose that He has desired since He was born. Unbidden, He weeps into this sweet silence, touched in places He has never felt before.

The Nameless One takes Him into His arms. "My beloved Logos, we are one! I, too, need to experience this journey, and through you this becomes possible. I send you forth into the realm of Earth so all may know me. You are the Light of the World; you are my voice made manifest. Together, we shall all return to the Celestial Kingdom and bask in the radiance of our completed journey." The Nameless One adds, "That is, of course until one of us desires another adventure!"

So intimately is the Logos embraced, so completely is He held in this space with no face, no form, and no substance, that He dissolves into the arms of the Father. He exults in praise, "Such is my love for you, my Beloved. Once I bowed down before you. Now, you raise me up, arms aloft. Smiling, you keep raising me, and now I look into your eyes. I stand before you, flooded with your joy! My heart breaks in every new moment!"

"Give me your self!" cries The Nameless One, innocently triumphant.

In radiant reverence, God-given giggles and intoxicated jumps of joy the Logos opens His arms and breathes an eternal *yes!* Then, with a sigh of ecstasy, He melts into silence and is gone!

Chapter 19

The Arrogant One

I sip my coffee just steps away the Demiurge's Headquarters. Situated in the stylish ninth arrondissement of Paris, this newly renovated art deco hotel has become the hub of the world's fastest growing online industry. I smile when I realize just how close The Louvre and Place de l'Opera are, knowing how Samael always insisted upon having prestigious neighbors.

I sit in an outdoor café, watching people come and go, looking to see if I recognize anyone, but I don't. I see mostly couriers, journalists, nerdy types and the occasional suit gliding through the golden swivel doors. On first impression, no one would know what really goes on behind those walls. The real and sinister agenda is cleverly concealed behind a glamorous veil of illusion. Yet soon, all that will change.

A black BMW convertible pulls up outside. Even through the tinted glass, I know it's Samael. A woman sits beside him, but I can't see who it is. I pull my sunglasses down, making sure I'm not recognized as I lean forward and watch him get out of the car. He stands tall and proud in a white suit and black shirt, running his fingers through his hair as he gazes up at the building. The woman, however, is struggling to get out of the sleek low-slung car. I watch her hoist herself up with both arms, one hand pushing against the windscreen and the other pressing on the roll bar.

"Get your hands off the car!" he roars. His voice is so loud I can hear him from across the street. For a second, a wave of shame passes through me, but I do not flinch. I remember how I must be impeccable with my emotional responses, especially now when I am so close to the Demiurge and its tempestuous archons.

Full of apologies, she cautiously teeters towards him, carrying countless files and bags, but he doesn't even help her. He just stands there brushing himself off and adjusting his suit before grabbing his MacBook from the trunk. She has to quickly step out of his way—otherwise he would have sent her flying. I look down into my coffee cup, trembling with emotion. Feeling saddened for the woman and furious at Samael's behavior, I stand up and place a ten-euro bill under my cup. Then I cross the road and enter the golden doors.

"I would like to see Samael please," I say to an immaculately dressed woman sitting behind a heavy baroque table inlaid with pearlescent cherubs.

"I am sorry, Mr Black is very busy. Would you like me to arrange an—"

I cut her off in mid sentence. "No, I want to see him now. Tell him his ex-wife is here, and that she is waiting." The receptionist looks around, expecting to see someone with me.

"I am sorry Madame, what is your name?" she asks.

"Tell him Sophia is here."

She picks up the phone and dials the appropriate number. She looks nervous. I can sense her heart pounding as she taps her fingernails against the varnished cherubs. I smile back at her, hopefully easing some of the tension that is clearly mounting.

"Bonjour Mr. Black, I have a lady waiting for you in reception. She says her name is Sophia." Silence greets her. Cold, empty, ever-expanding silence. "Mr Black ... Are you still there?"

I can't hear what is said, but I can feel the blow to his schedule.

"Yes Sir," she replies meekly before replacing the handset. "Mr Black will see you now. If you take the elevator to the top floor, you will find directions to his penthouse from there."

With an elegant nod, I walk across the octagonal entrance hall, consciously stepping on the black and white marble tiles that form a shiny chessboard on the floor. Black, White, Light, Dark, Spirit, *Matter, Masculine, Feminine. Life is an orchestrated dance of seemingly opposing opposites, until they all merge into one, and then there are none ...*

I can feel all of creation orchestrating itself around me: morphing, shape-shifting and penetrating the entire building. Everything is becoming more fluid and translucent. I am getting used to this perception of reality. The veil shimmers, and the seemingly dense nature of objects changes to my eyes. With relief and a growing sense of power I feel the ever-present weight of gravity lift and the general background groan of my once-human life quickly and completely dissolving.

I enter the glass elevator. The doors close, and seal me in as I ascend the backbone of the Demiurge, making my way to its creator at the very top. The higher I go, the more I expand. The doors open and I step out onto the top floor. There is a tremendous vibration in my ears as Light suffuses every cell. I now see everything as a hologram, a liquid light landscape capturing the most minute detail and far-reaching horizons. I follow the signs to Samael's suite. *I can feel him.* I can sense him breathing and he is not alone …

"I have made my choice," I whisper, holding my ground steadily. "I am staying until each and every soul has returned to the Pleroma. You can do your best to deter me, but I assure you that every soul you think you have destroyed, I shall save. With or without your nuclear disaster, this earth and every life-form on it shall live."

The Arrogant One glares at me as if filth has dirtied his French linen cuffs.

"Well, Sophia, you are going to have to do this all by yourself, because He is not coming back. Just remember that. Why do you linger here pathetically when there is no hope?"

Powerfully, I penetrate his eyes, diving deep into the nature of his being. I calmly speak the words he loathes to hear. "There is always hope."

He knows these words have a double meaning. He knows that I, his mother, also have hope for *him*, and this repulses him. He takes another step towards me, intensifying the already escalating situation. As he gets closer, he appears to tower above me. I remember that this used to really disempower me in the past. But not now.

He sneers above me. "Even if all that you hope for comes true, you will still have to taste the bitterness of mortality, for whether by the sword or by the slow decay of time, He will die. He cannot bear to be part of this world. He doesn't have the *means* to be here—unlike us. Remember Sophia, we have fallen, whereas He is still pure. There will be no comfort for you, no comfort to ease the pain of his passing. He will come to death, an image of the splendorous King in all His glory, undimmed before the saving of the world."

Samael rubs his hands together, savoring his words. He leans in closely. "But you, my *mother*—you will linger on in darkness and in doubt like nightfall in winter without a star. Here you will dwell, bound to your grief under the fading trees, until the world as you know it has changed and the long years of your life are utterly spent. There is nothing here for you—only death and loss." Samael appears to congratulate himself on every word. He is preening, proud of his epiphany, inflated by his own unquestionable prophecy.

I absorb his words, taking them deep into my heart and beyond. I am not deterred, and I take another step closer. I gaze into his soulless eyes without flinching. The sound of my own breathing echoes between us. Slowly, tenderly, I place my hand over the space where his heart should have been. We stand that way, suspended in time, transmitting unspeakable words and newfound emotions.

"Samael," I whisper. "You are still my son, and I love you with all that I Am. Yet still my choice remains. I am staying until every single timeline enfolds into none, and every soul has safely returned to the Pleroma, including you and all your creations."

I silently witness a boiling rage flare up inside of him, which he immediately reins in. With barely visible effort, he holds intact his perfected masquerade of elegant sophistication. I consciously maintain our wordless understanding of one another a little while longer, enough to make sure he tastes the unquestionable fortitude of my faith. I realize in compassionate epiphany that underneath his insatiable anger is the quaking fear of annihilation. For some reason, we know that this moment is inevitable. It is my destiny to do this—that is clear to both of us.

Seconds turn into minutes, and still neither one of us moves.

Unexpectedly, the effulgent loving presence of the Logos explodes into my heart, victoriously telling me that the Nameless One is aware of *everything*, and has sent Him back to Earth to help me fulfill my task. Suddenly I know Samael is wrong, and that my time here *shall* one day be complete.

Choirs of angels fill the room, but only I can hear them. Ecstasy races through my veins causing the irises of my eyes to open, sending torrents of love into Samael. He gasps and staggers backward; pulling a handkerchief from his top pocket he presses it against his mouth. His eyes are aghast with horror, because he has *seen* what I have seen and he has *felt* what I have felt, and he now *knows* that this is bigger than he initially realized. I disengage by gracefully lowering my eyes and turning my back on him as I walk out of his Parisian headquarters—and away from his insidious Empire for all time.

The sight of Sophia walking away infuriated him. It reminded him of the time she walked out on him before, leaving him alone sixteen months ago. He wished he could reach out and restrain her, grab her and squeeze out all the light from within her. Yet he maintained his composure until she was out of sight. Quivering with suppressed anger he returned to his private office. Once the door closed behind him, he released his pent up rage.

Like an aggressive virus, he replicated himself into everything that was as yet unformed, unknown, and uncreated. His exquisite French tailoring dissolved into a protoplasmic mass, oozing and smoldering from the fires of creation. Everything around him became subsumed, co-opted, hostilely taken over by his ever seeking and baleful glare. Within seconds his once enchanting eyes dissolved to reveal what was secretly lurking behind them.

All he saw, he became. All that was around him became absorbed by the gaping black hole that he was. All life was sucked into him. Instantly it became corrupted from its original perfect blueprint into a rambling, incoherent and degenerating mess. Everything in close proximity became entangled in his presence; all that was good in this world shattered at the touch of his gaze. Glorious moments of majesty imploded into dark mutterings of suppressed anguish; slumbering seeds of divinity were scattered before the wind of his wounded rage.

All those who succumbed to him lost themselves in the process. Everything became absorbed into his suppressed fury. Everything became part of the blanket of his shame, part of the balm of his hate. And still he continued to engulf all in his wake. For all Samael dared to see was his own self; anything other reminded him of *her* and everything she stood for. The thought of *her* evoked in him a yawning abyss of powerlessness, futility and rage. So, armored to the hilt with a fiery rage towards anyone who crossed him, Samael had become the monster he saw himself to be. He was his own self-fulfilling prophecy: un-wanted, unloved and cursed.

So he kept on creating, channeling his incombustible wrath into his work. His latest and greatest creation, the Demiurge, was proving to be quite a success. This web network was virtual—a completely "real" virtual matrix. Anything, *everything* one could ever imagine was available to experience in the Demiurge. This second Internet system was an epiphany of new and emerging technologies. This experience went far beyond imagination. In the illusion of the Demiurge, all was available to be actually felt and experienced—all five senses, the full spectrum of human emotions, and every conceivable fantasy.

Within the Demiurge, Samael created a wall of mirrors, so that everything reflected his own narcissistic splendor, his own vain reverie, and his own shameful soliloquy. He became a self-proclaimed god formed in his own image. By naming new things, he could claim them as his own, and by claiming them he made them in his own image. Thus, his Empire grew exponentially until almost every human being on the planet voluntarily plugged into his world on a day-to-day basis.

He imagined himself as untouchable as he wallowed in the glory and power of his self-proclaimed throne. The impenetrable charisma that cloaked him triggered both terror and fear, yet all were drawn to him by an insatiable attraction that always ended in a myriad of unsavory ways. This terror materialized into a dense fog, coating everything in its swirling veils of chaos, so that no one was able to see the ghost in the machine. Because of this, his Empire became strong.

The Demiurge's hugely successful advertising campaign was based on an artificial sense of human connectedness. Yet its true purpose was to slowly wean the human soul's natural longing for light away from its true Source. Samael's Demiurge was manufactured with separation at its core, specifically designed to divide and conquer. It fashioned myriads of forms that multiplied among themselves until separation from Source was the only reality, and all possibility of divine reunion was squandered and lost.

From these forms Samael had created seven Archons, seven agents of himself. From these seven children of his great aching wound came forth all the ways and means that Samael—the god of matter, the King of the artificial world—could manifest and sustain himself until the end of time. Like him, the Archons appeared as human beings, but they were flesh and blood bodies that masked a hideous lie.

The Archons were the great lords and ladies of suffering, skilled and perfected in their art of inflicting pain on others through deliberate and malevolent means. Subtle, powerful and undetectable they would influence the emotions of people, driving them mad with a barrage of darkened thoughts and vengeful attacks. Yet at first the Archons did not know how to use their innate talents, nor did they want to. Teeming with narcissism they showed only self-interest, preferring instead to turn their sabotaging attacks onto themselves and with one another. Delighting in his creations and their innate desire to maim, Samael taught them how to deliberately provoke other people, and to feed off of their emotional responses. To his great pleasure, in less than no time they had become masters of manipulation.

Over eons of history, the Archons became great kings, sorceresses, warriors and queens. Their ability to manipulate and confuse others, and then siphon energy from them, made the Archons invisible to the world—and even prolonged their lives. They never grew old, and neither did Samael. He showed them how they could gain power and wealth—and they loved him for it.

Without even noticing it, the Archons fell completely under the control of Samael. Horrendously addicted to suffering and pain, they gave all their power away to their creator. Afraid of losing their position as "Rulers" of humanity, they fell under his spell and did all his bidding, while he sat back and reaped the rewards. The more ambitious the Archons become, the more powerful Samael became. And the more powerful Samael became, the more he remembered who he was, and where he actually came from … And that *really* pissed him off. So he continued to create in darkness, in order to forget.

In a suite of the Demiurge's headquarters, high above the streets of Paris, they appeared out of the shadows. One at a time they stepped forward and claimed a seat at a shining glass conference table. Samael sat at its head, poised in his throne. His immaculate hands pressed against the glass, causing the highly polished surface to mist underneath them. He smiled as they assembled, and there was no doubt that when Samael switched on his charm, few could resist. Pleasure swept across his face, and he applauded once all seven were seated. His pride swelled and he spontaneously performed a standing ovation to himself and his creations. Then he walked around them, openly admiring their physical beauty and perfection.

"Ah, my dear friend Igor," he said, stroking Ignorance's shaved head, and looking deep into his eyes. "Yes! Perfect!" The eyes were a black mass with no light, no color, and the complete absence of anything but a blank stare that absorbed everything in its wake.

Samael walked to the next chair, where Wrath had already

become red-faced because he wasn't first to be admired. He had no self, no center, and no love at his core. The chip on his shoulder was huge, though he covered it with vitriol and smooth, sarcastic talk.

Samael gave Wrath a hearty slap on the back. "Looks like you forgot your blood pressure meds," he chuckled, unmoved by Wrath's reddening face and glowering eyes. Angered at his own perpetual annihilation, Wrath glanced at Igor, threatening him silently with a look of hideous rage as Samael moved away.

Greed eagerly awaited him, smooth and satiated in a well-cut suit with diamond cufflinks. He shook Samael's hand with a firm, slightly sweaty grip. This archon played with the big boys, consuming all in his wake, hording everything just to fuel himself, and growing larger from his own mad consumption. His well-groomed exterior was merely a sleek façade for the aching, gnawing emptiness within his own non-existent center.

Samael continued around the long polished table to the next of his creations. She was a slinking red-haired creature with long black fingernails. He examined her manicure, and then tossed her hand away, saying "I like Lust's nails better." Samael knew that his comment would set her off into a green fury, and it delighted him. Envy compared herself against everyone and everything. Inside, she was hollow with inferiority and pain. She despised anything that appeared more glorious. He loved her jealous sulking fits, her bitter comments and cruel barbs.

When Samael reached Lust, she drew a lacquered fingernail lazily along his thigh. His breath quickened with instant desire. This creation was so very perfect, and she had an intoxicating effect on him. She was deliciously dangerous, with her sleek dark hair, full pouty lips and luscious figure. Oh, yes, Lust had the power to seduce, to have him and claim him if he'd let her. Everywhere she went, she created sensation and abandon; she stoked the penetrating, smoky fires of sex, creating a craving so huge that its flames raged across the worlds.

Pride was the sixth Archon. He existed as the epitome of superficial arrogance portrayed as self-declared reverie, vanity, sophistication and elitist snobbery. Pride had stood up and walked to the window the moment Samael turned his attention to Lust. He had his back to the rest of the Archons as he gratified himself with champagne. As he sipped, he had a distant gaze in his eye, for he was secretly imagining ways in which *he* could become king.

Samael didn't miss a trick; he could smell the growing presumptuousness in the room and knew exactly where it was coming from. Stealthfully, Samael materialized at Pride's side. Fondling Pride's ear lobe between his forefinger and thumb, Samael rolled his eyes upwards as if to receive divine intervention before whispering into Pride's ear.

"What makes you think you are so special, hmmm?" The words insidiously found their way into the hollow space where humility should have been and burned into Pride's feelings of inferiority.

Pride responded by pulling on his own power as he stood his ground. "Because I am," he sneered back. "And you're the one who made me that way."

The room fell deathly quiet as the seven Archons looked on, eager to see what would happen next. Samael didn't disappoint them.

He took another step towards Pride, placing both hands on his shoulders and turning Pride towards him. "Sit down slave, like the rest of my subjects!" The sheer power of Samael's presence caused Pride's legs to weaken and buckle. With a shove, Samael sent him to his seat. Pride's growing feelings of humiliation were quickly masked as hate filled his being. The source of his pride and purpose of his being was the torpid contentment of feeling better than everything he surveyed. Yet in this humbling exchange, he had now become well and truly impotent.

The archons leaned back into their chairs, laughing at Pride's castration, secretly relieved that the tension was over, and that Samael hadn't attacked one of them. They took great pleasure in seeing another shamed. Samael flashed an icy glare towards the archons that commanded silence, as he sauntered over towards the last of his creations.

Sloth slouched in his chair—the inertia of nothingness, the ceasing, halting deadness of non-being and lack of enlivened purpose. From underneath a mop of dirty blond hair, a pair of lazy stoned eyes looked up at his master. A smile broke across Samael's lips. "Oh yes. Sloth. You are so uninspiring, so despondently futile, so utterly boring, that you almost depress me." Samael pinched Sloth's greasy cheek. "But not quite."

Sloth smirked at Samael's eloquence, relatively amused to receive some attention from his creator. Nothing really moved him though, apart from the deadening decline of all joy and happiness that constantly imploded into a depressing pit of inertia and despondency.

Samael roared with laughter as he turned his attention from Sloth. With his arms outstretched, he proclaimed to the company of archons, "You are glorious! Each and every one of you is an absolute masterpiece, if I do say so myself."

After the farce of greeting, the three-dimensional nature of the Demiurge's penthouse headquarters in downtown Paris melted away. The Archons' human skins shimmered and then evaporated. They became revealed in their full glory—autonomic in function and perverse in pleasure, steeped in sensation and designed for death. They stood proudly before Samael in his private realm, a canopied cavern hidden in the sub folds of space. A steaming slick of viscous, oily blackness coursed around him, perpetually folding and unfolding in upon itself; flickers of shadow danced around everyone in the absence of all light. Each of Archons bowed only to their king and carried out his bidding automatically, for they were living extensions of him. They did not breathe; rather they lived on what they absorbed from everything else. Like symbiotic parasites and vampires, they sucked life from the living. The Demiurge existed as their perverse playground, where there were no rules and no limit to their pleasures.

The meeting got fully underway. Samael raised his arms and proclaimed thus before the assembled archons:

"I am everywhere, in everything. I have created a world where I exist in all things. Let all my future and present subjects believe their god is everywhere and in everything. Let them believe they are gods and I their creator, and this realm is their sole existence. Let them believe they are free, free to be told what to do as I see fit. Let them believe this thought comes from them, and their own *free will*.

"I, King of the World, Lord of the Empire and all Dominions, do hereby proclaim myself divine. This is the dawn of a new day: the whole universe will recall it as the day of the new birth: the advent of the reign of the King of the Worlds!

I have existed from the morning of the world and I shall exist until the last star falls from the blackness of the night sky. Although I have taken the form of the King of the World, I am all men as I am no man; therefore I am a God!"

"They all love you, lord! They crave what you have created," came the spontaneous cry of Greed.

Lust parted her lips, "You are a god," she whispered.

Samael warmed to Lust's offering. Turning to face her, he opened his arms to emphasize his penetrating greatness. "Yes...and always am I Ruler: always am I he. Always am I unassailable in my kingdom. Nothing can touch me, as nothing else even exists anymore. I am all I see, and all everyone can see is me!"

"You are wise, just and true my Lord. Who can resist such magnificence," Ignorance spewed, almost falling over himself to deliver his compliment.

"Yes, yes, my Archons, it is true. BUT—this Sophia continues to profane my honor and glory! Her very name STILL lingers in the hearts and souls of humankind; why has she not been DESTROYED? She remains, despite my dealings with her. I WILL NOT TOLERATE THIS! All will acknowledge me as the one and only god, or they will ... simply cease to be." He spat his words out as he heaved with fury.

"I want you to continue annihilating her precious little humanity." They looked towards Samael, waiting on tenterhooks for what he was about to say next.

"Ignorance, Greed and Sloth you have spewed and multiplied yourselves magnificently into this putrid little society, and thanks to you, the foundations are set. Now it is time for Lust and Wrath to take over."

He walked over to where Lust was still sitting. "Your fifteen minutes of fame are calling, my child. It's time to release your special brand of Aphrodite into the market place. Let these sniveling, stinking worms gorge on your latest designer high. And Wrath, I want you to make them kill for it!"

Samael rolled his head back with insane laughter. "Let us create even more chaos. It is time to arrange a bigger and better catastrophe—one to make the Bay Area disaster look like a picnic! Yes, my Archons, let us create something that even *she* cannot put right."

The Archons smiled as they glanced around among themselves, snidely gloating at his last comment. Yes, they knew exactly what he meant by those last words. Aphrodite was a creation of Lust's, a designer drug that amplified every kind of sexual desire imaginable. Wicked and impure, the high gave way to the most taboo carnal acts of depravation. Her plan was to disseminate this drug into the club scenes of all the major cities in the world. The effects of the drug were hideous, creating a vicious instant addiction, so that the user would stop at nothing to get their next fix. Oh yes, the next phase of Samael's plan contained no mercy whatsoever. Giddy with worldly power, the Archons hid any remnants of their fear.

There were only two things that the Archons feared: Samael and the Logos. Samael had told them that if the Logos and Sophia were to meet, the power of their combined Light would become unlimited. They knew the Logos had the power to see into the unseen worlds because they saw Him there, bringing in His all-redeeming Light, destroying their systems and disrupting their plans. They also knew that once He found Sophia, His attention would focus on them. And in their collective gut they knew the game would then be over.

Their other fear was Faith. If someone had Faith in his or her own goodness and held onto that light within, the Archons were rendered impotent. These great beings of darkness didn't have any physical power against those who did not fear them. However, they could not be killed by ordinary means. Most weapons could not harm them, and any attack was instantly disintegrated. There was only one thing that could stop the Archons and vanquish Samael and his Demiurge forever.

And that was Sophia.

What She carried inside of Her held supremacy over them all.

Chapter 20

End of Days

I board the train soon after leaving the Demiurge Headquarters. I don't want to stay in Paris a second longer. For now, my mission is complete. I have stood empowered before Samael and spoken my deepest Truth, despite my molten rage over the catastrophe he has created in America. I am still elated and uplifted by the Light, yet my human body feels as if it is carrying the entire weight of the Bay Area disaster. I can't stop thinking about all those souls that have perished. It doesn't seem fair, and it doesn't seem just. I haven't had the chance to go online or catch up with the latest news, but by the look of the few headlines in the newsstands, it is not good.

Everywhere I turn, I feel my children—I see their faces and hear their cries. It's almost as if they are crying out to me from behind the veil, urging me to do something. But what? I slump into my designated seat in the train. It is seven and a half hours to Carcassonne. I close my eyes.

Immediately I'm transported back to the telephone call with Mom only days ago. *There has been an explosion at a nuclear power plant in the Bay Area and thousands have died. Sophia, radioactive waste is leaking out into the ocean and no one can stop it. Its terrible, sheer mayhem!* Her words ring in my ears.

Again I feel that something has been left undone, and that it is my job to complete the task. As my mind seeks the answer, I go beyond the day's events, leaving behind the drama with Samael and the fear of whether or not the Logos will truly return. I sink deeply into my consciousness. The rhythm of the train provides a soothing counterpoint.

I begin to spiral through countless mists and veils of supernal light until I eventually catch sight of the once-familiar contours of the Celestial Kingdom shimmering in the distance. In these last few days I have been awakening and remembering at a great rate. It all tumbles back now with pristine clarity.

At the Iron Gates of the highest and brightest palace of Heaven stands Saint Peter, holding the key that allows him to invite or prevent souls from entering Heaven after death. I see the customary congregation of souls queuing before him, patiently waiting their turn for the ritual he loves to perform. You can always guarantee a hive of activity at the gates; it's the ground zero for almost every soul coming face to face with the reality of life and death. Many of them fear to witness the three-minute playback of their lives, becoming terrified of its accumulative consequences. Many more fight it, and deny St. Peter's decision, leaving him with no choice but to hold the mirror of truth up to them so they see the actual condition of their soul. Others simply keel over and implode from the insurmountable grief of being separated from loved ones.

Only St. Peter can perform this role. No one else is able to handle it. Only he can stand there and bear the suffering, because he knows that it's the greatest of all initiations. He is so good at his role because he believes in it. Little does he know that I shall later lower my vast mantle over the battlements of Heaven, so that it flows across the Abyss and touches those who are suffering and dying on the dry and arid lands of this harsh, dark world.

All the souls who have been rejected by St. Peter the night before shall climb like ants up my mantle as I extend it to them in the grim darkness of the lower worlds. It is my role to make sure that every "rejected" soul shall bypass St. Peter and ultimately enter Heaven. I smile to myself when I remember how I would often overhear St. Peter, agitated and perplexed at being bypassed, asking the Nameless One what he should do.

Always my Beloved would reply, "Hush, Peter. Let it be." Then St. Peter would turn around and return to the gates utterly confused, and yet so profoundly comforted that a smile of pure joy would beam upon his face.

Then in a flash I realize this is it! This is what has been whispering at the edges of my mind all day! My eyes snap open. I suddenly know exactly what I am supposed to do—search for those souls lost in the disaster and extend my mantle!

So right there on the swaying train I search for them. There is no time to waste. The outer world recedes further, and I sink deep within the cavernous nature of my primordial self. Plunging and diving through the aeons, I lift up and scan the heights, calling and crying out for my babies. I have no conscious idea of what I am doing, but I am obeying the clamoring ache that propels my womb to find them.

I see them! They are clustered together, back-to-back, looking terribly afraid and so obviously lost. My heart extends towards them, transmitting an encircling wave of love and protective reassurance.

"Ma, Ma, where are you?" They feel me, they call to me and my heart instinctively responds by blindly rushing towards them.

Then from out of nowhere the Realm opens up, sending billons upon billons of creative sparks in every direction. A force like no other is here with us, and yet I do not feel afraid. I cannot sense who or what this is, yet it feels as if the whole of existence has turned around to watch me. I cannot move, nor do I want to. I simply marvel as the most glorious vision unfolds. Droplets of light begin to cascade towards the souls, who are now on their knees in songs of adulation. Stardust shimmers all around them as the mysterious presence slowly emerges before me.

In exquisite slow motion, I see the familiar tenderness of Her mantle extending. Slowly, slowly She unfurls Her vestment and extends the radiance of Her hem to the elated souls. Dancing motes of dust sparkle in Her gentle, grace-filled face; silver shines from Her chin and moonbeams spring forth from Her ears. Sapphire robes adorn Her one moment, crimson white the next. She is effortlessly beguiling; riveting, enchanting, wondrous! At last She turns towards me.

My heart stretches to oblivion in Her gaze. I know that Her eyes fill me with the absolute maximum amount of love that I can handle. If I were exposed to one drop more, I would cease to be. The extreme levels of Light and Love pulse through my being and push against the fabric that holds this incomprehensible story together.

Every part of me is trembling, every aspect hungry for this moment; every living, breathing creature that is connected to me rises up to catch a glimpse of Her face.

I am struggling to comprehend this moment. For Her face is my face … I am gazing at my Self. It is simply I, and I Am That. Countless realizations dawn and disappear as we exchange the transmission together. I see Her, and She sees me.

Gradually She extends Her arm towards me, Her alabaster fingertips glistening with goodness as I reach for Her. The instant we touch, ripples of supernal light surge through me with such vigor that I fear I may have to let go. On the edge of my consciousness I see Her lips move and hear the sound of my own voice in my head.

"You are my likeness…"

BOOM! Everything splits open. The impact of these words blows a hole in any place I imagined that I alone could not carry this burden. I AM NOT ALONE! In this quaking, evolutionary moment I realize things that cannot be spoken. They can only be tenderly integrated and then activated at the right time. Tears of infinite gratitude trickle from under my closed eyelids. My body shakes with subtle energy—I imagine I'm glowing.

Slowly I open my eyes to see a young girl in front of me, standing with a hand on my knee to keep her balance on the train. She and her mother sat opposite me on the journey from Paris. I wonder what they noticed, and I look at her with love, knowing she is one of my children.

"Madame we have arrived in Carcassonne," she announces in a small clear voice. "You are home now."

Her mother calls the child back to her seat, not realizing the pivotal role her daughter has played.

But I know her as a divine messenger. I wipe the tears from my cheeks with my sleeve. *Yes, I am home my darling. Home in every sense of the word.* Outside the station I hail a cab and head towards Puivert, my own Garden of Eden. By the time I reach Maison Rouge, I am ready to collapse. With a heavy yet jubilant body, I climb the stairs and fall into bed.

I wake to the sound of someone ringing the front doorbell. I roll over and reach for my bedside clock—argh, it's just after 10am! *My God, I must have needed that sleep.* I grab my crimson velvet cloak from the back of the bedpost, wrapping it around me as I descend the stairs. Just before reaching the door, I pause to raise the voluptuous hood of the gown. Then I open the door, not knowing what to expect, but ready for anything.

A vibrant grey-haired couple stands before me, looking as if they have seen the most wondrous ghost. I smile.

"My Lady." The man speaks first and removes his tweed hat. He places it in front of his heart as he gently bows.

The woman stands unashamedly gazing at me as delicate tears roll down her face. After several seconds, she also touches her heart with one hand, while her ring and middle finger lightly touch the space between her eyes as if to say *I see you.* Bizarrely, I find myself responding to her in the same way.

The woman holds my eyes with hers and says, "My Lady, we know who you are. We have waited so long for this moment." Her voice trembles. "So long, that at times we feared it may never arrive."

By now the old man has lifted his head and is looking skyward. The cobalt blue of his eyes shines, as if the color is lit from the inside. Tears roll down *his* cheeks as he speaks one simple word over and over again. "Merci, merci, merci..."

Profoundly touched, I bring my fingers to my lips to control the overwhelming emotions. My body quakes with energy as I stand there receiving their adoration. This is a brand new experience, one that I am rather uncomfortable with. Then a soft animal-like cry escapes from the back of my throat as I realize that these two are the first ones since the Logos to recognize me. To really see and know who I Am. I feel like keeling over as a wave of grief thousands of years in the making fills my heart. Reaching for the Logos in the inner realms, I call for His light to steady me. These electrifying revelations are not making me a kind and calm hostess in this moment.

"Please come in." I say with effort. Then I take a step backwards, opening the door wider so they can enter.

They sit together on the sofa holding one another's hands, while I go to the kitchen to make tea. I can hear them talking, reassuring one another, as they cry and giggle at what must be an intensely catalyzing moment for them. They look like they are in their late sixties, and they speak with a British accent. There is something about them that is teeming with life, yet they also carry a wistful timelessness.

While the water boils, I gaze into the garden as Samael's last words do their best to haunt me. *You will still have to taste the bitterness of mortality, for whether by the sword or the slow decay of time, he will die.* I shiver as I watch the magpies fight on the lawn for supremacy. *Wasn't the magpie the only bird that did not attend the crucifixion?* Although I have faith that the Logos will return, I can't help wishing that he would be here now to hold me. Yet *I am not alone.* Samael's old trick of instilling doubt is losing its power, for he does not know what I know and he has not seen what I have seen.

Soon enough he will come to understand that the darkness will not overcome the Light. Not because it can't, but because it doesn't wish too. At this stage he doesn't share these same understandings, and I do not require him to do so. But I wonder how much darkness he will generate before he does. Although eventually he will come to know it, as it is his nature, just as it was mine.

The teakettle whistles cheerily. I can tell already that today is going to be very important.

The couple's names are Leonardo and Martha. Over tea and biscuits, they explain that they live here in the region, close to a town called Tarascon, although they were both born in Scotland, hence the accent. They grew up in the area just outside of Edinburgh and knew at an early age that their parents were part of some ancient lineage, a kind of bloodline. As children, they thought little of it, but as they came of age, their parents and close friends held a circle to officially anoint them into the priest/priestess-hood. It was then they understood that their ancestors were the ancient Cathars of France.

They tell me that the Cathars carried on the teachings of Mary Magdalene and John the Beloved, who traveled here to Southern France after the Lord's resurrection some two thousand years ago. Earnestly they tell me that some say the Cathars were the offspring of our Lord and Lady, for His body did not die, and instead He traveled with Her in secret. For forty years He continued to live and breathe among them, sharing His teachings and initiating them for this very moment.

"And Now is the time," Martha says.

Leonardo continues, "You see, my Lady, we were told that you would return on the seventh year. For centuries we have prepared for your coming! Every seventh year we hold a vigil for your reunion. Many long years have passed as we waited patiently for you in the shadows, quietly passing our wisdom to our children, speaking of a great Lady who wears the crown of stars upon Her head. Calling back the Queen of Heaven, Whose tender mercy brought Her to us. Now, at last, we come to Her—to you." Leonardo leans closer. "Sophia my Lady, there is something we must do together."

Martha continues their narrative. "My Lady, we are aware of Samael and the power of his demiurge. We know about the disaster in the Bay Area, and we also know that he will be preparing for an all-out war against you. I understand that this is happening terribly fast—but we have been instructed to act now."

Here I interrupt. "What do you mean instructed? Who instructed you?"

"Well, we believe it was you, my Lady. Our faith speaks of how Mary Magdalene would often go into a trance and that you, the Holy Sophia, would speak through her. She told us of your descent, the creation of Samael and the Archons, the emergence of the Logos and the promise of everlasting life when you return to the Pleroma. Our faith is grounded in these teachings. And now we are living the teachings. The next step is of utmost importance!" Both of them look at me intently, with full faith.

Slowly I ask, "What is the next step?"

Leonardo's voice rings out into the room. "My Lady, you are to come out of the shadows, reveal yourself to the people and tell them the danger they are in!"

I take a deep breath and stand up. I can feel the rightness of this truth. Yet it is so huge. "How can I do that?" I exclaim.

Leonardo seems to have been waiting for this moment. With a flourish he opens his bag and pulls out his laptop and digital camera. "With this!" he declares. "Our grandchildren have told us this is the fastest and most direct way of getting your message out there. With their help we will be able to upload your video straight into the demiurge itself. You will appear on all the channels, and Samael's company won't be able to do a thing about it."

He winks at me confidently. "Our society has many talented ones. We are prepared to hack into the back system of the demiurge's main computer frame and covertly install the software that will disable anyone from being able to delete your message for at least forty-eight hours. By that time every person on every continent will hear your words."

"Our grandchildren know so much about computers," Martha adds demurely, with a twinkle in her eye.

I sit down again. My head begins to spin as I imagine all of the possible implications.

Martha comes to sit beside me. "My Lady. You told us at the beginning you would forget who you really are. We who have kept and remembered the teachings are here to remind you. Besides, whatever happens next has already been done. This has already been lived, and we are all here to simply re-enact this dance until each and every one of us remembers."

I nod silently, knowing that she speaks the truth. My shoulders grow heavy as I come to terms with the task upon me. I excuse myself and walk into the kitchen to contemplate my next move. I realize that this is going to cause huge, global, gi-normous waves, and that Samael is going to go quite crazy, in ways that even I may not be able to imagine. I walk towards the terrace doors, completely blown away by the series of events that have unfolded since I arrived in France. I stare into the garden, totally lost for words yet acutely aware of the razor's edge that I now stand upon. *Oh my God, this is so intense.* I gaze towards the lake. The light playfully dances upon the surface, sending sparkles everywhere. Children play in the water, splashing one another with cries of delight. I see their faces. They are filled with innocence and unbroken happiness. Something inside of me turns.

"Okay, let's do it." I stride back into the salon with a huge smile upon my face. "I am ready!"

Leonardo sets up the camera, explains what I have to do and leaves me to it.

I sit there staring at the camera, waiting patiently for the words to come. And they do.

"To the great men, women and children of Earth, I speak to you after searching my heart deeply. I have asked myself what seeds of wisdom have I gained to share with you, and what important lessons have I learned in my time on Earth. I have come up with two answers. Failure and Hope. These may seem idealistic and paradoxical choices, but please bear with me.

"Ultimately, we all have to decide for ourselves what constitutes failure, but the world is quite eager to give us a set of criteria if we let it. So I think it fair to say that by any conventional measure, I have known failure on an epic scale. After an exceptionally short-lived marriage imploded, I was jobless and as poor as it is possible to be without being homeless. Every fear that my parents once had for me, as well as every fear of my own, had come to pass. By any standard, I was the biggest failure I knew.

"Now, I am not going to sit here and tell you that failure is fun. That period of my life was a dark one, and I had no idea then how far the tunnel extended, and for a long time, any light at the end of it was a hope rather than a reality.

"So why am I speaking about this to you now? Simply because failure meant a stripping away of the inessential. I stopped pretending to myself that I was anything other than what I was, and began to direct all my energy into the only thing that mattered to me—waking up and living my Soul Purpose! Had I really succeeded at anything else, I might never have found the determination to succeed in my true mission. I was set free, because my greatest fear, utter failure had already been realized, and I was still here, and I was still alive."

I look intently into the camera, feeling the humble power of the words pouring through me. With a silent prayer, I continue. "You might never fail on the scale I did, but some failure in life is inevitable. It is impossible to live without failing at something, unless you live so cautiously that you might as well not have lived at all—in which case, you fail by default.

"The knowledge that you have emerged wiser and stronger from setbacks means that you are, ever after, secure in your ability to survive. You will never truly know yourself, or the strength of your relationships, until both have been tested by adversity.

"Now you might think that I choose my second theme, the

importance of hope, because of the part it played in resurrecting my life, but that is not wholly so. Hope is not only the fount of all invention and innovation—that uniquely human capacity to envision something other than what is, In its most transformative and revelatory capacity, hope is the power that enables us to go beyond our limitations again and again—and again.

"A great poet has said, 'Hope is the thing with wings,' and indeed we need our collective wings to shift all of the evils that humans inflict on other humans. Why do they do this? In their ignorance, people do it in order to gain or maintain power. I, like many of you, have had nightmares about so many things in this world that I have seen, heard, and felt. And yet—I have also witnessed more human goodness than ever before."

I straighten my back and let my voice ring out. "I am calling for the power of human empathy! I am calling for collective action! I am calling for ordinary people, whose personal well-being and security are assured, to join together in huge numbers to help people they do not know—people they may never meet. You see, humans can learn and understand without having fully experienced. They can think and feel themselves into other people's positions. I am calling on this faculty of compassion in all human souls!

"Of course, this is a power that is morally neutral. One could use this ability to manipulate and control, just as much as to understand and empathize."

I gather my forces and lean close to the camera. "Dear people, here is what I want to address most of all—the demiurge. The demiurge is a lethal distraction, being run by a very dark force. I know some of you will imagine that you are working with this dark force and that eventually you will be rewarded. I assure you—it doesn't work that way.

"Now, some of you may know about the nuclear disaster that happened twenty-four hours ago on the West Coast of America. The cause and aftermath of this event is being severely suppressed and diverted from the main news channels. This was a deliberate attack. It was planned by the demiurge to look like an accident. However, it was a purposeful, unprecedented upload by the demiurge's web network that caused the satellite to move off track, succumb to earth's gravity, and hit a nuclear plant in the Bay Area. Furthermore a dangerous level of electromagnetic waves affected all people plugged into the demiurge at the time of the attack. This too, was part of the demiurge's plan, because that level of Electromagnetic radiation causes a shutdown of people's empathic response in the frontal lobes of the brain. Empathy is the emotion that connects us all, and now many are left incapable of feeling it.

"This attack may be only the beginning. The demiurge was built on the foundations of arrogance, greed and fear. It seeks to dis-empower humanity and annihilate our intrinsic goodness. I believe that its founder will stop at nothing in his campaign against our very souls.

"Today I ask you to rise up with me and bring this demiurge to an end! Tell everyone you know, that the demiurge is an addictive distraction, a virus that is feeding upon humanity by degrading our social moral values and replacing them with a complete apathy for life. This is what is meant by the demiurge's most marketed slogan —*a worldwide web that surpasses reality*. The demiurge is only able to multiply more of itself. So that 'reality' the demiurge speaks of is merely its own - the ever growing hunger for more and more power."

I half expect Samael to come storming into the room. But I must play my part, as he must play his. Right now, I manage a brilliant smile, straight into the camera.

"To rise up takes hope. Your heartfelt action in the face of apathy will create a wave of hope around the Earth. Sometimes it is easier to avert the eyes, to choose to do nothing, rather than act. But I tell you with absolute certainty that even a small act of love will make a huge difference.

"The way you vote, the way you live, the way you love, and how you think will all make a difference. With your energy of hope, you bring enormous pressure to bear on the demiurge and any other oppressive powers operating in the world. You will have an impact way beyond your national borders. That is your privilege, and your burden.

"Dear ones, stand with me to bring the demiurge down and disentangle humanity from its grip. In the core of your being, you will know you have done the right thing. Our world is burning. Over half the population is now lost in the demiurge, and it grows more every day. Look around—can you see the change in our society? Can you tell that something is seriously wrong? People are wandering around with blank expressions on their faces, addicted to a false reality that is programmed to sap their very life force!

"Let us awaken again, and remember! Once upon a time we were radiant Kings and Queens of our beloved Earth. We do not need any special magic to change the world. We already carry the power we need inside ourselves—and the power is hope. I may appear to you as a woman whose body is small and feeble, but I assure you I have the heart and stomach of a Warrior Queen. Stand with me! There is nothing naïve about your impulse to heal the world. All it takes is one step of Love in Action—one blow against the insidious apathy of the demiurge—to send forth that tiny ripple of hope!"

By this time my whole body is alight. I am resonating with hope. I lean in to the camera and urge, "Send this recording to everyone you know. Let it go viral. Be unafraid, for I Am with you. You are never alone. A great rebirth is upon us. Turn within your hearts for wisdom and there you will find me."

I press stop. *That should do it*, I muse to myself.

The salon door slowly creaks open. The shining, radiant faces of Leonardo and Martha peer around the side. "Oh my Lady, that was outstanding!" cries Leonardo. "What a tremendous speech you gave."

Martha adds, "You have done it my Lady! Anyone with ears to hear shall hear you; anyone with eyes to see shall see you, for you are truly ablaze."

Leonardo packs the camera equipment away, and Martha takes me to one side. She explains that her grandchildren are on standby to play their role and that they will upload the movie later tonight.

"How did you know I would agree to this?" I ask her as we walk together barefoot on the lawn, enjoying the last rays of sun upon our skin.

"Because you said you would." She smiles. "It's part of the prophecy."

I fall silent. Worlds upon worlds rise and fall within me. Questions bubble up, only to descend again as wisdom soothes all curiosities. I slip my arm through Martha's, as we reflect on the day's events and the orchestration of forces that are now gathering at this epic time.

"You know there will be a response, don't you," says Martha.

"Of course," I reply. "Cause and effect—it gets us every time."

"How do you feel about that," she asks.

"Ready." I smile.

Chapter 21

Redemptive Seed

I cannot sleep. My heart lurches and my mind is in overdrive thinking of every possible scenario that I could possibly wake up to. Samael is going to go insane when he discovers what I have done. I have taken an irrevocable step—and in so doing I have jumped through the ring pass not. Come the morning, everything, everywhere shall be different. Tonight is not a night for sleeping; tonight is a night for fortifying my faith against his coming wrath.

I jump out of bed and grab my crimson velvet cloak. I feel like walking into the night, and being alone with the vast starry sky. If I don't get some perspective, I'm afraid my head will explode. I step outside to discover that the night is surprisingly warm. I walk along the path that heads toward the open fields overlooking the sheer cliff face of the valley. The moon is out. It's not quite full, but round enough to cast light upon my way. I can hear the owls hooting, both the male and the female, sounding their song from across the valley to one another. The moment I am outside, a great wave of peace suffuses me. Yes. This walk shall straighten me out.

I trample through the fields, which are strangely quiet. Usually

I can hear the cowbells of the herd clanging softly. I continue along the side of the cliff towards the ancient pathway that makes its way through the forest to the river down below. The sky is completely clear. Starlight and moonlight mingle in the air. In the distance I can clearly see the dark bulk of the Pyrenees Mountains. I stop for a moment to scan the skyline, knowing that the ancient stronghold of Montsegur is somewhere to the left of me, whereas up ahead I can just make out the warm orange glow of Rivel. Nearby, I feel the loving presence of Puivert Chateau, the old Cathar castle. My heart swells in adoration as I stand there marveling at where I find myself. *I absolutely love this place. How could I ever leave?*

After walking a little further, I find the gap in the cliff face that leads down into the forest. Treading carefully over the weathered rocks, I pick and chose my way towards a giant standing stone that looks as if it is covered in moss. The steep path down the cliff is littered with leaves and pieces of twig that crunch and crumble every time I take a step. *I am not exactly being very quiet*, I giggle to myself. But it doesn't really matter, as there is no one here except me.

I clamber onto a large standing stone. It looks like a menhir, an ancient rock that would have been used to mark the site of religious ceremonies. As I stand up and walk towards the edge of it, I realize just how far the drop actually is. *This place is incredible.* I can see the whole, valley, from the river down below all the way to the moon up above. I stand in wonder, feeling pure grace descend into my whole being.

The balls of my feet press into the glistening moss. Instantly, powerful waves of pleasure soothe my troubled mind. My toes caress the cool moist carpet, gripping and releasing clumps of gorgeousness. The rock grounds me and connects me to the energy flowing through it. My inborn ability to merge with nature seduces me. I soak in the atmosphere of the midnight forest, reveling in the sounds and sensations that beckon my surrender and invite my nakedness. I want to feel the moonlight on my belly, the soft breeze on my awakening skin. I slowly untie the soft velvet cloak from my shoulders and release it to the mossy rock. My skin quivers as the cool night air caresses the entire length of my back. Closing my eyes I breathe deep into my heart and fully relinquish all concern for the coming days. What will be will be; it is part of the eternal and perfect plan.

The aromatic fragrance of pine and cedar fills my nostrils, sending primal waves of excitement rushing through me. I breathe in deeply, desirous for more as the tension drops from my shoulders. Inhaling and exhaling, my body fills with the healing gifted to me by the elementals in this beautiful moment. Aroused and tingling with nature's force, I am hungry for more. I stretch up my arms and turn around to see the majestic silhouette of Puivert Chateau standing proudly. The chateau, too, is a sacred fortress. It reminds me once again to draw strength from this land. Grateful for its presence, I emotionally reach towards the Chateau, filling myself with its strong and true vertical masculinity.

Instantly, my heart is replenished with an incandescent fire, and an all-body longing rampages through me like a wild bull. Amplified bliss surges through my veins, causing my body to tremble with desire. I stand upon the giant menhir in my billowing silk negligee. The elementals respond by playfully picking up the cloak at my feet and dropping it on the forest floor.

Coyly, I remove one strap of my negligee from my shoulders,

imagining with a delicious shiver that one hundred eyes are upon me. Savoring every moment, my fingers instinctively wander over my breasts, concealing them in the cup of my hands. The other strap of my negligee drops, and the silk slips to the lowest part of my hips. With a tantalizing wiggle, I make it fall to the soft moss, and I step from it completely. Fiercely aware of my nakedness, I slowly raise my head to gaze up toward the treetops, so I can drink from the moonlight that is drenching me. Ecstatic fire ricochets through the center of my spine. Of their own accord, my hands slip from my breasts and down the curve of my body to the white-hot fire of my naked fertility.

I am quivering with eternity's sensual touch, feeling my soul unite with the pulsing lifeblood of the infinite. My vision expands to see time multiplying its endless mightiness and joy into the delighted souls of all lovers communing on Earth at this moment. In the union of above and below, they are suffused with the passionate heartbeat of undying love, drenched with a sweetness that can never fade. This immoral moment belongs to those with rapturous hearts and eyes who arch ecstatically towards the translucent perpetual calm.

My passionate words resound through the forest. "Oh Great Mystery, you reveal yourself and yet remain forever unfathomable. I declare before You that this New World shall be born from my suffering! The ashes of my tears shall dissolve to become the drink of your eternal life! Come to me now, Nameless One, for I dwell in this holy body temple, and I shall eternally guard the mystery of the world!"

My prayer rises from the deep, and impregnates me with a volcanic heat and strength. Deep authority ignites within me. I open my arms to embrace the night, and part my legs to unbridle the full force of my birthing power. This action causes my whole body to quake with orgasm in a way that I have never known before. I groan with irrevocable pleasure as the limits of my physical body yoke with my prayer. I acknowledge the divine resurrection of my sexual force stirring within the depths of my feminine nature.

Beads of sweat form upon my brow as I continue this soulful activation. With insurmountable command I speak to all the powers of creation, knowing that every single one is listening. Most of all, I speak to the people—the souls upon the earth, the souls within the earth and the souls that surround it. These are the countless beings forming the whole of humanity. They are an inter-dependent force, born to awaken in this evolutionary moment.

Standing proudly upon the menhir, I breathe deeply as the blazing trinity of Love, Power and Wisdom dance within me. As the trinity unites, it shoots a laser of potent creative force right through the center of my spine.

Again I call out in prayerful exhortation. "People of Earth, hear me! I am Sophia, the She-ness of All-That-Is and I walk amongst you. What many of you have heard is true! The darkness has gathered around you—even as I speak, it is already within your homes.

"Believe me when I say we have a difficult time ahead of us. There will be a great many who give their lives to this cause. But I say to you—they do not die! For they shall rise victoriously into the new life that awaits them as we continue birthing into the New Dawn. The demiurge will try everything within its power to rein us in and get us under its control again. But we must first shed our fear of it as we prepare to enter the Great Rebirth that is coming!

"I am truthfully unafraid. Why? Because I remember. I remember that I am here not because of the path that lies before me, but because of the path that lies *behind* me. I remember that since the beginning of time I have been here and I remember that which matters most ... I *always* shall be! Beloved humanity, do not let the demiurge make you forget that you are eternal Souls! Let us unite as one, irrevocably connected with the Source of all love as we walk away from the demiurge and awaken into the light once again! Let the power of our collective decision tremble this planet of earth and stone! Let us be heard from red core to black sky!"

As I stand commandingly in the moonlight, the elementals spiral around me, amplifying my message and sending it out through the ethers. My whole body is shaking with energy and sweat drenches my skin. This unexpected initiation has made me ablaze with life. Suddenly I cry out with pleasure and grab the nearest tree, as a second wave of primordial orgasm surges through my legs before rippling out into everything. I close my eyes, drop my forehead against the trunk and breathe deeply. The coarse bark presses against my face, distracting me for a moment before another subtle wave of sensation washes through me. I cling onto this ancient forest guardian, listening to my own breath in the soft and potent night. For a long while, I drift in and out of various realms of consciousness.

I do not hear the footsteps of an approaching stranger until ... *Snap! Crunch!* They are very close.

I am jerked into the present. *Something* is here. I open my eyes but do not move. I strain my ears to listen for an identifying sound or voice. *Crunch! Pant! Sniff! The footsteps are getting closer, and there are more than one!* My breath is barely audible. I extend my subtle awareness out, feeling the space in-between us, reading the energy of the new arrivals. *It's a man and a large dog and they come in peace.*

"Who are you?" I question, and take a couple of steps towards the sound. Uphill at the edge of the clearing, I see a figure step into the moonlight. He is broad, tall, and confident. His presence fills the natural archway. I make no move to cover myself; I care not about my nakedness. I am She, the primordial Feminine. The moonlight shines in my face, blinding me from seeing his features.

"Speak your name," I demand. He does not answer, though I know he is watching me. I see the vapor of his breath against the cool night air. From out of the shadows a large dog appears and sits beside him. In unison they take a step forward, and I notice that he is wearing a hood. He is still hidden, shrouded by mystery, and yet I feel so comfortable with the situation. "Why do you hide from me? Why are you here?" I ask, as I energetically open myself to him.

"I am here to protect that which matters most," the man whispers.

I gasp in wonder. I *know* that voice. "Logos?"

He takes a step closer and pulls back his hood. "Yes it is I. But touch me not for I am still descending. If you touch me now the process will stop." His breath catches in his throat. "My Beloved, the magnificence of your light is overwhelming! I beg you, my Lady, please turn away for a moment. The glorious sight of you is more than I can bear."

Turn away! My heart feels as if it is being torn in two. I want nothing more than to rush towards him and feel the warmth of his body upon mine. I have been longing so intensely, so desperately, for him! After our first and only kiss, he left me reeling with Love and aching for more, yet in the next moment he was gone! Since then I have not stopped thinking about him, wondering when he would return—and *if* he would return.

Now he has asked me to turn around! How can I turn from his beloved face, the face I yearn to kiss, and the body I am hungering to hold? Yet I also understand the process of descending onto Earth; I know the pain he speaks of. I know the feeling of being shredded and compressed as pure light diminishes into matter. Reluctantly, I turn away from him, praying that he does not leave.

Oh! Now I hear him coming closer. My breath quickens as a titillating bolt of anticipation shoots through me. The dog, or rather the *wolf* begins to howl at the moon. Together they are an exquisite mix, a blend of shamanic, tantric cosmic-ness. I swoon when I feel his warm breath upon my right shoulder. His heat causes my nipples to protrude and lift. My heart thumps against my chest and the incessant ache in my body grows stronger.

"You may not be able to touch me my love, but I am able to touch you," he breathes in my ear. I gasp with delight as I surrender to his touch. My head rolls towards his chest and I inhale his deep, rich fragrance.

I shudder with delight at his touch. He makes no insinuation and utters no sound, but we communicate perfectly. His familiar touch and smell fills me with life. I long to share my boundless love and femininity with him. Close and inviting, his breath calms my trembling nerves. The slow rise and fall of his chest speaks to me.

His powerful presence radiates between us. It ignites my inner flame, and I feel the Divine fire melding our souls. I close my eyes and feel his many hands touching me, and his many mouths tasting my skin. I want him to be fused with me, from mouth to feet! I want to climb inside of him and end this madness of separation!

Slowly, he pulls my hair from my shoulders before whispering into my skin. "I have always been with you. I have whispered your name in the rustle of the leaves of autumn; I have called to you with the voice of the waves of the sea. I have watched you while I hid in the clouds. The birds have sung my messages, and I have given you echoes of my presence through all eyes that have looked at you."

I feel as if I am going to burst. His love is magnifying mine and my body is too small a container. "I have ached from our separation my Beloved, for I love you and long to give you life. I am so filled with this Love, yet I have no place to put it!"

"That is not true Sophia. Send your love and desire out into the world. May our redemptive seed rain down upon the souls of humanity. Love each and every one of them as you love me, and this, my Queen, is how our Heaven shall come to Earth."

And so I do. I make love with the elements. I make love with the night. I make love with the day being born. The more he ravishes me, the more I crave his touch. And in this primordial darkened world I learn how to transform my cravings into creations. I rise and fall, like the most tumultuous ocean as his kisses penetrate my flesh. His hands reach for mine and pull me open. I am like a desert thirsty for water. Our ecstasy rises to a crescendo before peaking at a level I have never experienced before. The Logos, the living word, masterfully guides our energy into the finest realms of consciousness as he speaks a language of Light that only I can decipher.

Afterwards, as we lie close on the forest floor, he tells of his ascent and his return to the Pleroma. He tells of how he was asked to return to Earth. He whispers of the Nameless One's longing, and His devotion to me and his understanding of my journey. He describes the Pleroma and everything he saw there, taking his time to highlight the details so I can see through his eyes the home I long to return to. On and on he speaks, bringing me with him through his recent journey. Through his voice and words, I see the Nameless One; I feel His love, and taste His longing. The Logos' deep and loving voice opens the gateway for me to enter, where my birthplace awaits me on the other side.

By the time he finishes I am just starting to shiver with cold. The Logos bends down and picks up my cloak, wrapping it around me and taking me into his arms.

He looks deeply into my eyes. "There is still something else I need to share with you." I can feel his chest expand as he takes a deep breath of the night air. Then he presses his lips into the base of my skull, releasing his breath in a warm blast. My eyes widen in surprise as the velocity of his light pierces straight into my brain, shooting cascading transmissions into both hemispheres. My body goes limp and the Logos holds me steadily. My vision soars free, unshackled from my body.

I am in a cave, and there is a woman before me. I walk closer and realize it is Pythia, not in the present day, but from a time in the distant past. I hold my breath as Pythia lowers Her eyes and begins to whisper strange words: words I cannot comprehend or recognize. My heart pounds. Something potent is about to happen. Adrenalin pulses through my veins as Pythia continues to utter a dialect that intoxicates and enchants me. Her words become louder and faster, as if conjuring up a once-forgotten emotion. Her energy charges the cave, creating an electrifying intensity of expectation. Suddenly She throws her head back and stops! I can see the whites of Her eyes. Deafening silence encircles us. Then She shouts, "Stay alert— no matter what happens!"

Through the half-light of our diminishing fire I notice Her breathing seems cumbersome, as if the toll of Her burden was almost too much to bear. In reverent silence I watch over Her, waiting for Her to return to normal consciousness.

"You are the custodian of the Holy Order, and they shall come to you in their droves." Although Pythia's lips move, I hear my own voice speaking. "There will be times when they shall believe in you more than you believe in yourself. During these times they will foresee the threats upon the horizon most clearly! In your heaviest hour you will feel as if you are fighting your own battle against the dark nature of your power, in the pursuit of some greater good. THAT IS THE TIME TO CLEAVE TO THIS MESSAGE!" *I gasp as the heat of these words scalds my own throat.*

Pythia's eyes return to their normal gaze. She suddenly smiles with a warmth so generous that I feel uplifted beyond measure. "Gather yourself Sophia, for I have something else to tell you."

I sit up straighter, as She adds more logs to the fire. Then She stands up and wraps her black woolen cloak around Her to cast out the cold from Her bones. She rubs Her hands together. I wait and watch. Head bowed, She paces around the cave before striding towards the entrance, filling the opening with her silhouette. She lifts up her hood, pulls Her cascading curls to one shoulder and returns to the fire where I sit.

She keeps Her voice low, and Her face shrouded, as She tells me that almost all of the recorded history of the Holy Order was written in the warm, wet blood that poured from the swords of their insatiable conquerors. These conquerors seeped poisonous propaganda into the realm, hoping to keep the Order paralyzed in exile, unable to establish another fortified stronghold. The Order, She stresses, was far from being a terrifying sect; they were truly good and decent people. Men and women who knew that one day I would return and that they would be ready to serve me—body, heart and soul.

She continues to speak of how the Holy Order are the torch bearers of Humanity—the Poets, Seers, and Saints, who shall lead the race out of darkness towards the Light. Without them, Humanity could lose its way in the impending darkness. She tells me how they honor all of Life: communing with the forces of Nature, treating men and women as equals and having no use for money from their congregations. They heal the sick with herbs and with the spiritual essence that radiates from their hands whist living in the servitude of Unconditional Love. They have a profound understanding of life and the human body, and though their ancient inquisitors say they despised life on earth, it is truly only the Demiurge they despise.

"Sophia, they knew of Samael long ago." Her eyes rest on mine, watching me closely. "Samael has been around a long time, much longer than you may realize. The demiurge has had many faces, many agendas—but always the same goal."

I nod for Her to continue.

She explains that The Holy Order knew it was Samael behind the Demiurge. They knew he was gravely misusing the forces of nature for his vampiric greed of power, wealth, and control of the masses. They vowed long ago to restore the balance, no matter what it took. They had nothing to lose, as the material world meant nothing to them. There was no hook that the demiurge could cast into them—and this infuriated Samael.

I am leaning in closely, hanging onto every word. Pythia describes how The Holy Order was the last of the original souls, human beings that had not become separated during the descent of darkness. These precious few bestow hope for the rest of humanity, as their connection to the Source is still relatively intact. Through consistent discipline and practices they maintain a direct and intimate communication with The Logos, while teaching others how to retrieve their souls from the Demiurge's bottomless pit of empty promises.

She tells me, "You have already met two members from the Order—Leonardo and Martha. With your message you will meet many, many more."

For a moment my mind works frantically, as more pieces of the puzzle slot into place. "The Cathars were ... and are part of the Holy Order ..." This isn't so much of a question, more of an answer. A beautiful pattern is growing in my understanding.

In the background, Pythia's voice continues. She speaks of the birth of the Troubadours, performers and musical mystics that brought about the concepts of chivalry and courtly love in a time when marriages were arranged only for wealth and power. Marriages like these kept the Demiurge in its prime position of power. "Divide and Conquer" was its strategy. Its desire for control was further distorted by the sadistic plan to wipe out the natural impulses of love and truth from the within the structures of human DNA. This would eradicate once and for all the human hope and longing to return home. Home has two meanings, I realize: home with the other half of one's soul, and home within the everlasting realm of the Creator's Love.

There were those who remained caught in the demiurge's

propaganda, and still feared The Holy Order. Yet the Troubadour's message stirred their hearts, heralding the message of revolution and igniting the once forgotten dream of staging a possible revolt. That message came right from the beating heart of Puivert—the chateau that still to this day proclaims that very same message. A light goes on inside my own mind. That is why I am here! To reignite the Chateau and restore its former glory as a centerpiece of evolutionary awakening!

Pythia reaches across the fire and grabs my hand. "The energy within the Chateau has the power to rise up as an epicenter of Light. After all, it was designed for this. Its source of power is being drawn from the earth's movement within the tectonic plates. Sophia, you have to know how to tap into it! The last time this happened you witnessed the last two hundred Cathars move towards the smoking pyre, which was their earthly completion.

"As they walked towards their victors, their voices rang out as one harmonious song with each other and to the One. This song was not a voice of fanaticism or martyrdom, but one of understanding. For they knew that three women and two men had escaped the consumption of the flames.

"One at a time they looked towards you before stepping into the fire, for they knew they did not face death, but instead would reunite with you on the other side of the veil. And because of their faith they sung out in adoration, knowing that The Holy Order was safe to live on."

Silence fills the cave.

"Sophia, even as we speak the Order is stirring. By the time morning arrives they will be making their way towards you. Prepare the Chateau, for the time has come!"

Her last words still echo within me as I am thrust unmercifully back into my body. The Logos still holds me untiringly, despite the shaking and convulsing of all my limbs. His presence soothes me, ironing out excessive energy from my nervous system. With one arm he holds me close, while the other hand orchestrates the download of my vision into full integration.

"She spoke of Puivert, the Chateau," I whisper. "It is to become the epicenter of … my ministry."

"My Lady, it has always been your place on Earth," He replies. "That is why you are here once again." I look towards the Chateau. In the pre-dawn it now looks more magnificent than ever. More and more pieces slip effortlessly into place as the Logos and I rock gently in the breeze. I feel like I can stay like this forever, but a wave of tiredness is beckoning. The Logos senses my withdrawal and helps me on with my negligee, wrapping me warmly within the cloak once again.

"There is just one more thing I wanted to share with you," he says. "The Nameless One knows of how Samael came into being. He knows of the demiurge and the creation of its rulers, but, to my surprise, it does not faze Him. It's as if He knew of this all along!"

I smile as my eternal love for Him swims through me, lapping against the shores of my heart. The Logos's words anoint me with such sweet medicine. He may imagine that he is the messenger of my Beloved, but to me they are one and the same.

I gaze out towards the horizon as I contemplate his words. "Did He speak of how we would do this? How we would bring glory to the End of Days?" I ask.

He whispers tenderly, "My Beloved, I believe I have just showed you."

Chapter 22

Enthronement

It is day. I am alone, yet the power of last night sings through every cell of my body. I feel as if I am slowly becoming more Light than flesh. As I walk to the village in the sunlight, the valley of Puivert opens up before me. I pause, momentarily drinking in the Eden-like scene: soft emerald lowlands down below, the Chateau standing guard at my left and the hazy foothills of the Pyrenees at my right. I can hear the local farmers in their fields, the children running for the schoolbus and the birds singing about the glory of late spring. It is the strangest feeling to know what I know—and to continue on as normal. It seems like any other day, but for me it's the day after the night before.

In a fleeting moment of nostalgia, I wish I could be a "normal" person—one who could just take the whole day off and spend time at the lake swimming, reading and getting a tan. But now I know who I am, and like ashes in the wind, my carefree days are gone and lost forever. *Would I exchange all the wisdom and experience I have gained?* I muse. *Would I throw it away for a day at the beach and a few fleeting pleasures?* I shake my head in amusement. The answer is clear.

As I walk into the village, my cell vibrates in my back pocket. It's Leonardo and Martha.

"Hey there, good morning!" I cheerfully answer.

The buoyant voice of Leonardo fills my ears. "Good morning my Lady! I have wonderful news to share with you! Your message has gone viral, and not just within the demiurge, but all over the Internet. AND ..." He pauses for effect. "It has been picked up by some of the news channels, including CNN and BBC!"

"What?" I exclaim. "Have you seen it?"

"Yes my Lady. Martha and I have not slept properly since we left you. We have been filled with a new lease on life. Everything is quickening! Needless to say our communication channels have been red hot since you gave your speech. We have been inundated with telephone calls from our members, as well as a deluge of e-mails from people after they saw your movie.

"Sophia, Beloved Lady—it is happening. The people have heard your message and they have taken it to heart. The time has really come. We are so filled with gratitude ..." His voice trails off and I feel his deep emotion even through my little phone.

I stop in my tracks and take a breath. I lift my eyes and gaze over the valley as a wave of gratitude also fills my heart. Rays of sunshine penetrate the clouds, and send sunbeams of heavenly light across the fields. I realize with finality that my human life is thinning and this fills me with a medley of emotions.

"Er ... my Lady, are you there?"

"Yes, yes I am here. I am just taking a moment to let this all sink in," I reply.

Leonardo goes on to explain that I need to record another message. All the people who responded had one question: now that we are awakened to the mission, what is the next step? I fleetingly wonder the same thing, and then agree to make a second movie later today. After we discuss the time to meet, I sense a change in Leonardo's energy.

"My lady, there is one more thing … Never mind, I'll explain when I get there."

I am curious, yet calm. They will meet me at Maison Rouge in an hour, and all shall be revealed. I continue to walk towards the post office with the intention of sending my parents a postcard. How normal! It all seems so bizarre, as if I am living two lives— One as a daughter who has fled to France to sort her life out, and the other as some kind of Savior-ess who is being flashed across the news channels. *The news! Oh God, my parents! What if they see me on TV?*

I suddenly realize the extent of my actions. Though I know I have made the right choice, it may be a huge shock for those close to me. I pause for a moment to contemplate this, yet there is nothing I can do to change or soften its impact. I hope they can understand; it's only a brief matter of time before they will know what I'm up to, if they don't already.

An hour later, I open the door to an exuberant Leonardo and Martha. The elderly couple looks positively younger, larger and filled with life.

"My, my, my you guys look amazing," I tell them. "Come on in!"

Our second meeting feels like a reunion of old friends. We sit together in the salon, while they excitedly share their news of the last twenty-four hours. They speak about the covert operation of hacking into the demiurge, and how, with seconds to spare, they managed to upload the video before a power cut struck their neighborhood.

Hummm, interesting, I can easily guess who was behind that. I find myself surprised to be so calm. Samael doesn't terrify me the way he used to.

I bring my attention back to Martha and Leonardo, who are telling me about the thousands of messages they've already received. People are responding from as far and wide as Africa, Australia and China! I listen in silence, absolutely astounded by everything that I am hearing.

"What about you my Lady? What has been happening for you?" asks Martha.

I exhale nervously, wondering whether I will tell them *everything* that happened last night, or just go with the edited version. I settle for the edit.

"He is here?" Leonardo gasps.

"Not quite—nearly." I tell them. "He is still in the descension process. He said that he would be with me …"

"In three days!" Leonardo cuts in. "And that is tomorrow."

"Er, yeah" I reply. I am surprised he knows this.

Martha looks earnestly at Leonardo. She whispers urgently, "It is time. You have received the answer to your prayer. The confirmation has been given. She met with Him last night."

"My dears, would you mind telling me what is going on? Please," I entreat.

Leonardo readjusts his position in the chair and gazes straight into my eyes. He reminds me that tomorrow is Pentecost. Leaning forward, he tells me intently that this is the day the Prophecy speaks of as being the day of my coronation. According to the Holy Order, on Pentecost Our Lady received the Holy Spirit. At that time She told the disciples that in the seventh year She would return and be made Queen. Her coronation not only signifies the receiving of Her crown, but also heralds the beginning of Her spiritual mission on Earth.

"The beginning?" I cry out. "I ... I have done so much already! Haven't I already started? At least a little," I amend, looking at their sweet earnest faces. Suddenly I feel foolish.

"My Lady, forgive me if I speak bluntly. You, er ... You are currently in the divinization *process*. It may be rude of me to say, but ..." He looks awkwardly at Martha, who nods in encouragement. "You are still at times very much human. The final completion happens when you receive your crown. And *then*, your mission begins."

My heart fills with love as I smile back at him. "Touché," I whisper. "I didn't think you would notice." We all burst out laughing, especially me. The sound of their amusement makes me laugh even harder. My face aches from smiling so much. I beg then to stop, although I secretly love every single second of this divine comedy. A lightness sweeps through the house, bonding us even closer and birthing a new understanding between us.

"To the great men, women and children of Earth, I speak as one who knows well the situation that we are now facing. I have searched my heart and soul for the right words to uplift you, the right energy to inspire you, and more importantly than any of that, the right guidance to liberate you.

"I have come to realize that the full spectrum of our human capabilities will be required to dispel Samael's shadow from humanity. To your ordinary eyes, I may look like a little blue-eyed, passive, sweet person who goes along with whatever happens and meekly accepts everything imposed upon her.

But I know you have eyes to see, and that my outer image could not be further from the truth.

"For countless years I clawed my way to this position so I could speak with you today. I learned during these years that we cannot and *must not* exclude the dark aspects of the feminine—Her majesty, power, passion *and* heartbreak. This acceptance of the dark is the catalyzing force that not only grounds and roots the divine light into our hearts and bodies, but also restores the balance and justice of this world.

"I personally know the one who is squandering our Earth and harming humanity. And as the power of the Feminine, I am filled with molten rage at his actions. I am furious at the horror that has been created. I am heart-broken at the lives being lost in the Bay Area disaster. I am heart-broken about the nuclear waste pouring into the ocean from this explosion. Dear people, my heartbreak does not end there. I am heart-broken about the two billion people living on less than a dollar a day, unable to raise their energies above the grind of survival. I am heart-broken at the disappearing forests; I am heart-broken that two hundred species vanish every day off the face of this Earth.

"People of Earth, if you are heart-broken too, then please be brave and strong! Stand beside me and hold some of this heartbreak. Then make a commitment within yourself to do something about it. Together, we will stop this insanity.

"We must not be afraid of our anger! It has its place in galvanizing us to action! We must raise our collective voice and say NO to every imaginable type of injustice! I tell you now, in the voice of the Wild Feminine—*use* the chthonic forces that manifest within! Feel the thrill of restoring balance, no matter the cost! This will fill your lives—and mine—with inner meaning and purpose!

"Know that my revelation to you is a revolution. It's an evolutionary revolution that calmly demands the transformation of all terms and conditions of life on earth. It is a gigantic wake-up call! I remind you of the total sacredness of the universe and the absolute sacredness of every human and every other sentient being sharing Earth with us. Dearest humanity, we have the absolute responsibility to enact that sacredness in a way that will potentially change the entire experience of life on earth. Earth is destined to change, and humanity along with it.

"Dearest Friends, please quietly and calmly take in what I am now about to say." I look intently into the little video camera and take a breath, exhaling light and strength out into the world. Then I speak.

"The time has arrived to awaken and remember our divinity! Each of us lives with a spark of divine Love, Wisdom and Power within our hearts! The time has come to claim this Divine birthright!"

I lower my voice and say with intensity, "Samael Black and his demiurge are hell-bent on destroying our capacity to remember who we are. If we stay locked into the demiurge, the window of opportunity may arrive, but we won't even notice it. We will remain entrenched within the demiurge and our magnificent chance will pass us by. Nature and her inhabitants will sail into a glorious rebirth, whereas we will inevitably die, glued to our plasma screens as we feed the entrails of the death machine!

"Along with everything else, humankind is constantly evolving. Soon we shall reach a point where we cannot continue in our current state of ignorance and disconnection. So, in many ways we can bless the creator of the demiurge for initiating this evolutionary crisis, because he has brought forward our choice point: Do or Die.

"He has set in motion a ruthless orchestration of events and energies that have attracted the attention of those who are heavily invested in the harmonious balance and well-being of Earth. These very energies of destruction are here to awaken us! I suggest very strongly that we work with them, rather than against them.

"My Beloved humanity, I tell you truthfully that dedicated and ecstatic love is the only response I find honorable in this tragic and desperate crisis the demiurge has created. You may be thinking, *how on Earth can we be ecstatic at a moment like this?* Because, my dearest friends, Love is the most powerful tool of transformation we have. Whatever happens, whatever horror or destruction unfolds now upon the world, however terrible the suffering becomes, a loving and ecstatic response will keep the heart open, the energy flowing and the thrill of courage and compassion alive. This is what is needed to liberate us all!

"Perhaps the most terrible and shattering schizophrenia that haunts the human race is our religiously imposed hatred of the body and our religiously imposed dissociation from the holy powers that sexuality can express. One of the greatest gifts I wish to share with you is how to see, know, and feel our bodies as sacred temples of divine love consciousness. We can consecrate our deepest desires without overpowering, dominating or exploiting others. We can make love in a tender, humble, rapturous celebration of divine love in action. I know we can learn through grace how to love in this way, with our radiant minds, impassioned hearts, and fully awakened bodies!

"Dear lovers, as you learn to love in sensitive, rapturous celebration, you will be flooded by a holy energy—the sacred tantric power. With that golden energy humbly and radiantly bubbling in your veins, you will be able to take on whatever tasks are needed to reverse this tragedy and birth our new world!

"Without a tantric revolution at the heart of this rebirth, there *will* be no rebirth! Only by the complete blessing of the body and the consecrating of the body's desires into tantric adoration can we ignite the latent potential in our DNA. Divinized sexuality will become the pioneering force on Earth! It fuses matter and spirit most quickly and intensely. Our willingness to love in a new way will lead us into a great evolutionary adventure!

"To pioneer a new humanity, we must claim ourselves as both sexual *and* divine beings. I ask you, how would one have the bravery for such an epic journey without the great fuel of divinized sexuality? The journey of evolution is tremendous, devastating, glorious and heartbreaking. It is the tantric force that lights the flame and passion of the divine human. All reality, in all levels, is indeed the tantric Beloved!

The time for the complete restoration of the mystery of divine Eros is here! This needs to be the image that now burns in our human hearts.

"Both halves of the tantric pair will be inspired to do impossible things and to fulfill their unique destiny on Earth. Tantric pairs of lovers will demonstrate the new humanity: a lucid, sacred intellect married to a loving, self-aware soul, married to an explosive passionate heart, married to a divine body irrigated by naked love fire! This, my beloved friends, is the vision of what the real authentic divine human being can be!"

I lean into the camera, engaging it with my eyes. "I speak to all the women listening now. Within us lives an immensity of love that is the great alchemical power of the universe. Men desire to experience it in its pure essence, and we need to experience it in the same way.

"All of us who will comprise the new humanity—women *and* men—must love one another so completely that we give fully to each other, and we give all to something *greater* than each other. This kind of love can lead us through total madness, to total revelation. We can expect to be totally shattered and totally remade in this deep commitment, and I promise you—we will also become the living vessel of the greatest miracle in evolutionary history! Through grace and through the passion of your love, you will become the sacred vessel known as the Holy Grail!

"My friends, this divine alchemy is your birthright—and it is what the demiurge seeks to destroy in you. Samael Black wants this power so badly. But it cannot be taken, only offered. And I am afraid Samael will first have to experience love in his own heart for the miracle to happen.

"As I come to the end of this second message, I ask that you cleave to my words and hold them dear in your heart. Begin to activate them in your unique, God-given ways. Be unafraid, for I am with you, along with many others. I am here to ignite within you the full divine love consciousness in radical action. I offer this as a gift, for I ... I am—"

Something catches in my throat. I can't quite say it. Quickly I conclude. "I am a voice of feminine radiance and power. Once again, please help this message to go viral. There is not a moment to lose! No matter what happens in the outer world, the great Rebirth is upon us! Turn within your own hearts for wisdom and that is where you will find me."

I lean forward and press stop.

Like clockwork Leonardo and Martha peer around the door nodding solemnly as they sit down in front of me. Leonardo speaks first. "I understand that it is difficult for you to actually come out and say who you are."

"I can't do it Leonardo," I whisper. "I just cannot find the words to say it." Inside I feel that I have let them down, that I have I let myself down. "It feels totally impossible to say those words— 'I am Sophia, the Goddess of Wisdom!' What if this is some kind of mass delusion that we are all falling for?" I turn my eyes from his and hang my head in shame.

Martha reaches over for Leonardo's hand, "Its okay love, just give her some time."

"But we don't have time, Martha. She *has* to believe in who she is! She cannot receive her crown if she still has lingering doubts!" Leonardo gets up and walks to the window.

I lift my eyes and watch him standing there, feeling his many dreams and prayers being shaken at their root. I feel terrible, absolutely heartless and blinded by confusion. I look over towards Martha who is staring at her husband, silently praying for his courage and fortitude.

Then my perspective shifts, and I am looking at myself from above. I see a small human form with a great weight upon her shoulders. I see how alone she appears to be, and how these strangers believe in her so tremendously. I see her parents in Toronto, worried senseless for their daughter's safety, and I see the many ordeals and challenges that she has had to endlessly face and overcome. I see too, how far she has come. There is only one small step left ...

There will be times when they shall believe in you more than you believe in yourself. During these times they will foresee the threats upon the horizon most clearly! In your heaviest hour you will feel as if you are fighting your own battle against the dark nature of your power, in the pursuit of some greater good. THAT IS THE TIME TO CLEAVE TO THIS MESSAGE!

The words from last night clamor in my ears. Tears prickle at my eyes, as I acknowledge for the first time how tired I am, how exhausted I feel from this journey. I look back and see the whole path: the memories of my childhood as an only child growing up with mum and dad, discovering my only solace was in the woodland with the animals. I see my awkwardness at being human, the discomfort of being here, the longing for something more, the yearning for my real home. I see how inauthentic I was in relationship; how this thing called love was nothing like Love as I remembered it. I can feel the gaping hole in my heart that occurred when I realized just how far from home I had traveled, and that I had no idea how I could return. I can see now in hindsight, that my attraction for Samael was one based on primordial memory. Being with him, I had a sense of family and so when he asked, I jumped at the chance to marry him. For a few fleeting moments it was truly glorious, a stupendous reunion that made life on Earth almost bearable.

And then it became a supreme ordeal, some kind of hellish nightmare that almost crushed me to a pulp. I inwardly recoil as I remember how merely the sight of one another opened wounds that were strictly off limits—wounds that we imagined were unredeemable. We fought and collided day and night, and yet still... I love him. I love him as my husband and I love him as my son. And I realize with a jolt that I will do everything within my power to save him, even as he attempts to destroy the world.

"My Lady, are you okay?" Martha's soft tones penetrate my memories.

From some deep place inside of me a voice answers: a voice suffused with faith that has been paradoxically restored by the love I have for Samael. "Yes Martha I am okay. I am ready to do this."

Leonardo walks over and gives me a bear hug. "It's not impossible to tell the truth to someone ... who already knows." He gives me a wink.

There will be times when they shall believe in you more than you believe in yourself.

I step out of the bath and return to my bedroom. The room flickers in candlelight as I dry off and rub scented oil on my body. I stand in front of the windows overlooking the Chateau. From where I am everything appears to be the same. The Chateau looks like it always does, an old Cathar castle perched upon the hillside serving as a reminder of times gone by. And yet, in a few hours time, I shall be standing there in the courtyard under the cover of midnight to fulfill an ancient prophecy, one that I apparently foretold many, many years ago.

I slip into my dress, one that my mother gave to me: one that was given to her by my grandmother. I remember when I was packing for France I saw the dress hanging in the back of my closet. It was one that I would occasionally wear if I were going to a fancy dress party. For some reason I decided to bring it, imagining that it might come in handy, considering the reputation that France has with fashion. I fantasized about wearing it to the opera, in the kind of event one sees in the movies—ladies head to toe in their finest adornments, elegantly sipping champagne while a man in a tuxedo whispers untold desires into her ear. But I never could have imagined its current purpose.

Swathes of royal blue silk enfold my anointed body. The back of the dress plunges into a deep V with ruffles of blue silk that cascade over my hips before dropping like liquid light onto the floor. One gossamer thin layer of raw silk forms the slash neck that barely touches my décolletage, hinting at the nakedness underneath.

Mom told me that it was a vintage dress from the early 1900s, a dress originally worn by some exotic Dutch dancer turned spy. Apparently this woman was the first free-spirited bohemian and seductress to achieve "celebrity" status. She was known for her great strength and personal courage. Her style exuded opulence and luxury, and she was also known for her love of jewels, especially ornamental arm wear and headpieces. I can feel her strength, beauty and courage permeating the royal blue silk.

"It's just perfect," I say to myself, as I turn in front of the mirror.

I go to the dresser to select my jewelry. I don't actually have much to choose from. There's a selection of feathered earrings, some large gold hoops and a more inconspicuous pair made from rose quartz and turquoise. After some time trying them all on, I decide to not wear any.

It's the same with my hair. I have spent all afternoon figuring out what to do with it: should I wear it up, should I wear it down, should I braid it? In the end, I decide to let it dry naturally and wear it lose and unruly.

Once the dress is fastened, I stand back and look at myself in the mirror. My reflection is quite stunning, a striking apparition of freshly washed red curls that tumble over deep oceanic folds of royal blue fluidity. I sigh to myself in a moment of peace and satisfaction. The dress is simply gorgeous, and the more I turn to admire myself, the more I realize that without even noticing, I have truly grown into someone who looks like a real Queen.

It's time to leave.

I place my cloak around my shoulders and pull my hair free. I have decided to walk barefoot through the fields towards the Chateau. I had discovered an old *sentier de troubadour*, an original pathway the troubadours used to reach the castle. By taking this trail, I will avoid the roads and the village down below. I close the door behind me and take a very deep breath. The evening air is still warm from the sun, and suffused with the fragrance of honeysuckle and jasmine. I walk through the *hameau* like it's any other evening, wishing the occasional neighbor a good night as I pass.

The way leads straight into a luscious emerald field that is soft and sensual under my feet. Every footstep sends waves of delight through my body as I pass unnoticed around the back of the village, towards the Notre Dame church where the ancient pathway once famed by the troubadours lays waiting.

The moment I step onto the path, the energy changes. There are trees on either side of the track that form a canopy overhead, and the further I go the darker it becomes. I pick up the train of my dress and look down to choose my path carefully. Some of the stones are smooth and well worn, while others are jagged and rough underfoot. I have to move carefully because on either side of me brambles are eager to get their thorns into my flesh or catch my hair upon their branches.

Up above, I hear the sound of owls calling across the valley. The male one is close to me, up ahead in the trees. I pause for a moment and hear the response from the female somewhere in the distance. Ghostly shapes emerge on either side of me, forming huge megaliths that flank the path. The scent of evening flowers and fresh fields begins to fade, replaced by the pungent smell of damp earth and something old. I open my arms so my fingertips can brush against the slabs of smooth stone that tower over me. My breath changes the instant I touch them. A bolt of lightening flashes overhead, sending shivers of thrill and ecstasy through my veins.

The elements whirl around me, shape-shifting my perception and heightening my every sense. The more I climb towards the Chateau, the more I am filled with an incomprehensible power. Thunder strikes overhead, sending evocative memories crashing through my mind. As I twist my way along the path, I heave and groan, not because of effort or tiredness, but from sensual delight and deep bodily feeling. I have the same sensations as from the night before. I feel like a radical revolutionary force making love with her surroundings. Every step becomes more orgasmic as I near the

Chateau. Somewhere ahead of me I hear a ceremonial chant of invocation that turns the air thick with echoes from the past.

Thunder and lightening sound all around me, but no rain comes. The closer I get, the louder the chanting sounds. Suddenly I find myself in a clearing. Immediately the chanting and thunder stop. I stand very still, not knowing where I am. The heady scent of smoldering frankincense assails my nose. Through the plumes of sacred smoke, I can see that I appear to be in the courtyard of the Chateau. Potent silence sounds in my ears, despite the thunderous pounding of my heart.

I hear a voice. "Draw nigh, O powers, visible and invisible: You, who are carriers of the Sacred. Draw nigh, cover your eyes and hush, For the Presence of the Beloved is at hand."

Someone approaches me from behind. I cannot see who it is, but it feels like Martha. "Come with me," she whispers, and gently guides me into the center of the courtyard. In front of us, a large shape emerges through the clouds of incense. As we approach I realize that it is a throne, carved from stone and marked in symbols. To the unseeing eye it would appear as a large boulder, or a kind of hunting chair commonly seen in the local forests.

A woman standing by the chair indicates for me to sit down. Tentatively I reach forward with my fingers to gauge the height of the seat, and unexpectedly brush against an embroidered velvet cushion. I turn around and slowly sit down. I can now see the shape of the woman, but a veil conceals her face. As she crouches down to adjust the train of my dress, I can see the flickering of blazing torches move closer towards me. The light from the flames obscures the faces of the people while amplifying the darkness of night. All I can see is a world of black and gold.

Before standing up, the woman anoints my feet with strong smelling oil, whispering words that barely reach my ears. As she rejoins the circle I look down and notice that she has formed a half-moon of rippling fabric and flowers at my feet.

A figure approaches me. I have the feeling that it is Leonardo. He is carrying something in his arms.

"My Lady, is your Majesty willing to take the Oath?"

Without hesitation, I reply. "I am."

"Are you Sophia, Our Lady of the Heavens?" he asks.

"I Am."

"Do you swear to uphold the prophecy and to rebirth the Kingdom- Queendom on Earth according to God's Holy Order?" he asks.

"I do, so help me God." I reply.

"Are you the Holy Sophia, the Great Mother of us all?"

Again I answer, "I Am."

He solemnly bows before me, then takes another step closer. Despite his proximity I still cannot see his face, but I *know* it is Leonardo. He proceeds to place an orb in my left hand and a scepter in my right, before kneeling on one knee before me. I can feel great emotion rising in his chest, which in turn triggers my own.

I am shaking and trembling, as waves of energy course through the throne. Out of the corner of my eye I look down to see veins of light shimmering around me to form some kind of rotating kaleidoscopic hologram. As I gaze up towards the sky I see the same swirling formation brewing above me.

As above, so below.

From his kneeling position the man throws open his arms and turns his face skyward. "In the Mystery of the Radiant Mother of the World, and of Her Consort, the Logos, we beseech Thee, O Divine Origin, beyond all thought or description, to accept these gifts which we humbly offer unto Thee." The light catches his face and I see clearly it is Leonardo, transformed in ecstasy.

"Beloved Presence, Whose body illumines the Sacred Gate. Bridge across the Stars! Beloved Presence, Keeper of the Crossroads: Awaken our hearts to the holy vision that bridges the visible and the invisible worlds, Always with us, yet not always seen. Open our hearts to Thy touch!" The voice of Leonardo resounds across the courtyard, and beyond.

He whispers, "My Lady, place your left hand before me."

I rest the orb on my lap and reach my hand towards him.

He takes it and places a ring on my finger. I notice tears in his eyes as he says in a powerful voice, "By this ring I anoint you, the Holy Sophia. Our Queen has returned—the redeemer of our souls. O glorious Mystery! Heaven's holy Tremors resound on Earth! For in Thy reunion Thou hast come, The Two-in-One ..."

An explosion of thunder collides overhead, causing the whole congregation to gasp and look up. Above us a swirling mass of red purple clouds spew forth particles of light that rain down like luminescent nighttime snow. Leonardo pauses for a second to take in the spectacle before continuing with the ceremony.

"Now in His eyes will shine Thy Glory, and in Her eyes the wonder of life regained: The ensouled and the ensouler, Face to Face and sealed by the bridge to the Most High!" The heightened emotion is detectable in his voice, which quavers with feeling.

The congregation in the courtyard now moves as one. Together they form a slowly gyrating mandala, while sounding a low continuous pitch. A feverish intensity builds about us. All around me the hologram spirals and morphs as the dance of light mirrors itself in all other dimensions. Unknown realms of existence become solid apparitions that reflect mere wisps of dreams: tangible, palpable, fluid light ripples like waves at sunset, coalescing on the shores of space itself.

As the thunder and lightening continue to boom and crackle above us, something in me is torn asunder. Like the molten propulsion of virginal lava that bursts forth from a sleeping volcano, an enormous voice inside of me breaks free from its cage and soars to the surface.

I stand and speak.

"I was sent forth from the Power, and I have come to those who reflect upon me. For I am the First and the Last. I am the honoured one and the scorned one.

I am the whore and the holy one—I am the wife and the virgin!"

An electrifying current passes through the courtyard sending shockwaves through the congregation. At the same time, a blast of light illuminates the Chateau. The swirling mass above us has now opened to reveal pure daylight behind the clouds.

He is coming!

I cry, louder than the thunder, "When you find me here, you will live, and you will never, never die again!"

The heavens open up, sending forth a pillar of effulgent light that anchors itself deep into the earth of Puivert Chateau. Its impact causes the congregation to stagger backwards, while I am thrown unceremoniously back into my throne.

An unearthly sound fills our ears. An otherworldly light glares before our eyes and then disappears. Darkness swallows us, as the impact from the explosion extinguishes our flames.

There is nothing—no sound, no movement, only the jagged anticipation within my own breath. I stand again, and as if in a dream, I am pulled to the place where the pillar of light descended. Before me from out of the blackness comes He! The figure of a man created from my Beloved's heavenly light. The Logos! I stand before Him in radiant Love. We are encased in Light.

Leonardo rubs the particles of dirt from off this face, and gets up to check on Martha. A little bit bruised, but high on endorphins, she smiles radiantly in the direction of her husband. She jumps up and runs towards him. He catches her in his arms and spins around and around in elation.

"It is happening!" he cries over and over again. "It is happening!"

Dazed and confused, the rest of the congregation slowly emerges from the shadows.

"My darling, look!" cries Martha.

She points him in the direction of The Holy Sophia, who is now drenched in glistening, shimmering, glorious black light whilst the Logos is ablaze with the golden particles of Creation. From within Him, the Logos forges a crown and places rubies and sapphires from the womb of Sophia into the headband. Together they drop to their knees, as a celestial choir sounds all around them. Awe and wonder fills the courtyard, as a corona of supernal light eclipses The Holy Sophia and The Logos.

He gently lowers the crown upon Her head and says, "This crown has been forged by the fires of our Love. It was, is and ever shall be a symbol of our redemptive seed! This seed shall scatter itself upon the face of this Earth. For I am The Logos, and my word is the Living Light of the Nameless One. And by this crown, I declare to you ... The Grail King has returned!"

RETURN
OF THE
GRAIL KING
Part Two: The Logos' Story
VERNAL EQUINOX 2015

HEIROS GAMOS

Part Three: The Great Rebirth

VERNAL EQUINOX 2016

Afterword

This novel contains numerous quotes taken from the *Ritual of the Bridal Chamber: The Gnostic Mystery of the Eucharist*, © 2004 Rosamonde Miller, History of Copyrights 1981, 1984, 1990, 2004 by Rosamonde Miller as well as quotes from the following *Gospels of the Holy Order of Mary Magdalene: the Testament of John*, "He flew to Her" and *the Testament of Miriam of Magdala*, "My meeting with Joseph." © Rosamonde Miller, 1983. Those and others can be found at www.marymagdaleneshrine.org, www.gnosticsanctuary.org. These include the quoted portions in the following pages.

Page 4 taken from the *Invocation, The Gnostic Mystery of the Eucharist*, page 1:

> Out of the Fullness came He, Who, without speaking, yet spake His name, and it was unknown to all but Him. And She, Whose womb is the gateway to all the worlds.

Page 33, 34, 35, 42, 68, taken from the *Surrender, The Gnostic Mystery of the Eucharist,* page 3:

> I have been apart and I have lost my way. The Archons have taken my vision. At times I am filled with Thee, but often I am blind to Thy Presence, when all I see is this world of form. My ignorance and blindness are all I have to offer, but these I give to Thee, holding back nothing. And in my hours of darkness, when I am not even sure there is a Thou, hearing my call, I still call to Thee with all my heart. Hear the cry of my voice, clamoring from this desert, for my soul is parched, and my heart can barely stand this longing.

Page 96: taken from the *Passion, The Gnostic Mystery of the Eucharist,* page 6:

> And the Logos answered: They say I came for all, but in truth, I came for Her Who came for all.

Page 126, 241 taken from the *Consummation, The Gnostic Mystery of the Eucharist,* page 13:

> O glorious Mystery! Heavens holy Tremors resound on earth. For in Thy reunion Thou hast come, The Two-in-One. Now in His eyes will shine Thy Glory, and in Her eyes the wonder of life regained: The ensouled and the ensouler, Face to Face and sealed by the bridge to the Most High.

Page 215: taken from the *Bridal Feast, Hierophantic Blessing, The Gnostic Mystery of the Eucharist*, page 14:

I have always been with you. I have whispered your name in the rustle of the leaves of autumn; I have called to you with the voice of the waves of the sea. I have watched you while I hid in the clouds. The birds have sung my messages, and I have given you echoes of my presence through all eyes that have looked at you.

Page 137, 138 taken from the *Gospels of the Holy Order of Mary Magdalene*, www.marymagdaleneshrine.org, *the Testament of John, He flew to Her:*

He flew to her. Through the spheres he passed and though each sphere he passed. Yet in each He remained. From each sphere He took its nature and yet, the integrity of the Fullness He retained. Between each sphere He remained, and yet He continued His journey. Joining the worlds was a heavenly bridge, whose beauty would light the way for all who could see.

Page 133 taken from the *Gospels of the Holy Order of Mary Magdalene*, www.marymagdaleneshrine.org, *Testament of Miriam of Magdala, My meeting with Joseph:*

The indignant word never left me, for the clearest eyes I had ever seen, eyes imprinted in my heart since my earliest childhood, stared right at me: The eyes of an angel, loving and reassuring, seen while I was an infant, still bundled in swaddling clothes.

Page 239: taken from the *Welcoming, The Gnostic Mystery of the Eucharist*, page 8:

Draw nigh, O powers, visible and invisible: You, who are carriers if the Sacred. Draw nigh, cover your eyes and hush, for the presence of the Beloved is at hand.

Page 240, 241: taken from the *Consecration, The Gnostic Mystery of the Eucharist*, page 10:

In the Mystery of the radiant Mother of the World and of Her Consort, the Logos. We beseech Thee, O Divine Origin, beyond all thought or description, to accept these gifts, which we humbly offer unto Thee. Beloved Presence, whose body illumines the Sacred Gate; Bridge across the stars. Beloved Presence, Keeper of the Crossroads: Awaken our hearts to the holy vision that bridges the visible and the invisible worlds, always with us, yet not always seen: Open our hearts to Thy touch.

Sources and Resources

The Gnostic Mystery of the Eucharist and *The Gospels of the Holy Order of Mary Magdalene* by Rosamonde Miller

The Gnostic Gospels by Elaine Pagels

The Gospel of Mary Magdalene by Jean-Yves Leloup

The Nag Hammadi Texts

On The Path to the Holy Grail by Antonin Gadal

The Pistis Sophia by G.R.S. Mead

ANAIYA SOPHIA is the author of Sacred Sexual Union, Pilgrimage of Love, Open Your Heart with Kundalini Yoga and coauthor of Womb Wisdom. She lives in southern France with her beloved, in a mystical Bed & Breakfast in Puivert known as AmmaRosa. Stay up to date with all her writings and events by signing up to receive her monthly Love Letter.

www.anaiyasophia.com

www.ammarosa.com